CHOICE, CHANGE

CHANGE

From Crime to Christ.
The Milton Campbell Story

by
MILTON CAMPBELL

Edited by Derville Lowe

Cover Design and interior layout by NCH Publishing
nchpublishing.godaddysites.com

Books by this author are available on Amazon, through
booksellers or by contacting:

Milton Campbell
Montego Bay, Jamaica
campbellmilton415@gmail.com

Norwood Creative Hub (NCH) Publishing
British Columbia, Canada
norwood.creativehub@gmail.com

CONTENTS

PREFACE

Early one morning while sitting on my bed, I recalled a conversation I had with one of my relatives who was living overseas, about my life's journey with Christ Jesus. The conversation motivated me to write this book about my life and the transformation I experienced by accepting Jesus as my Lord and Savior.

I want you to pay close attention to what I will share about my life's journey and the transformation that took place. It was 10:30 pm one night when I had a conversation with my cousin because I was dead broke. I asked him to help me out, and at that moment, to my surprise, he asked me if I was a Christian. Yes, I am! I replied. He started laughing at me, then said the most shocking thing – "you should ask Jesus for what you need because I worked for mine".

This was my little cousin who was dishing out this type of harsh treatment to me. I was so hurt by his profanity and disparaging comments that it brought tears to my eyes. The Lord saw my plight and said to my heart - I will inspire you to write my words to my people and out of it you shall eat bread; you, your mother, brothers, and sister.

I was a wretched man before I found Christ; my life was a living mess. I respected no one and did to people what I pleased. I lacked knowledge and always thought I was right in every situation. Little did I know that the path I was on would only lead to destruction and suffering, but God stepped in.

God's words are powerful, alive and active; they have the power to transform lives. When He speaks, light breaks through darkness, demons flee, mountains are moved, hearts are changed and old becomes new.

This is the story of my transformation from darkness to light.

DEDICATION

———

First and foremost, I want to give God thanks for the many blessings he has given me over the years and for the things He has allowed me to experience that brought me closer to Him.

I am dedicating this book to my mother - Marcia Jones. I want to thank her for raising four boys on her own. You put in the hard work, made the sacrifices, and did the best you could with what you had.

After all the trouble and heartache that I caused you, you were still there for me. Mommy, I pray that this book will help me financially to secure your dreams.

Thank you, mama! You deserve the best in life.

ACKNOWLEDGEMENT

All praise and thanks to The Almighty God for his love, mercy and grace extended to me throughout my life. I am undeserving of His matchless grace, but through His transforming power, I have been lifted to higher ground where I am now standing in the faith, grounded and steadfast. I am determined to do His will and to make a difference in the lives of many.

To Pastor Glen O. Samuels and the team at the West Jamaica Conference of Seventh-day Adventist, who has been instrumental in mentoring me and helping me to grow spiritually and engage with the church and community.

Pastor Charles Brevitt also played a mighty role in my life; always wishing me the best and supports me in many ways with gifts and books that would help my spiritual growth. He's real supportive in my life always telling people about me and where God has brought me from to where I am now in my life.

I also want to extend my appreciation to Derville Lowe, who made the choice to give me a chance, by editing and publishing my book. He helped me bring my dream to life and to the world. This has brought a meaningful change in my life.

Special thanks to Mrs. Fray for always being a spiritual guide to me in my time of need. She was a mother and a mentor throughout my incarceration.

Thanks to all those who said I would never come to anything good; you all gave me the fuel to prove you wrong. I turned all the negative energy into something positive. This is proof of what God is able to do for you.

Never allow anyone to tell you that you can't accomplish your dreams and that they're too big for you. I am happy that I heeded God's call and allowed the Holy Spirit to work in my life and transform me into the man I am today.

"But may the God of all grace, who called us to His eternal glory by Christ Jesus, after you have suffered a while, perfect, establish, strengthen and settle you."
- 1 Peter 5:10

CHAPTER 1
A Troubled Youth

―――――

The spell of darkness gripped my life at a very early age. At the age of fourteen, satan took full control of my life. I started holding up and robbing school children at knife point. I started becoming notorious at my school - the Glendevon Primary and Junior High (formerly Glendevon All Age). The children started becoming fearful of me because of my attitude toward them. I quickly became an apathetic young man with a pernicious mindset toward humanity.

I remember attacking a boy with a knife while in grade nine and injuring him badly, resulting in my expulsion from school. Due to my behavior, I was barred from enrolling in other schools no matter how hard my mother tried. The teachers and principal of my school believed I was an outrageous, disgraceful and scandalous monster, who brought shame to the school. At the tender age of fifteen, the outlook for my future was not promising and there was no help for me in sight.

Owing to my bad behavior, I was unable to enroll into another school, so I turned to a street gang for refuge at the tender age of sixteen. Little did I know that my life was about to change for worse. I started to do things that were unbelievable to my mother and father and all my loved ones. I started staying in the company of friends who were older than I was, but of the three of us, I was the deadliest.

We eventually became involved in gang feuds with other gangs from inner-city communities in Montego Bay. I was fighting both young and older men alike; some could have been my father. My mother and father were worried sick about my safety, but I was fearless and careless because the devil was telling me that I was untouchable; that I couldn't get hurt and that I was protected by him. I was worse than cancer and AIDS combined.

Together, we were a force to be reckoned with in the streets. We started robbing school children from the inner-city schools around town and we soon expanded to other parishes. My fame started spreading and all my friends were calling me "BJ" - the great gun kid. The feuds with other inner-city street gangs started to worsen and people were now getting badly hurt. Families were burdened with the cost of hospital bills and other costs. Persons were being stabbed, chopped, and burned with acid. The shooting would soon follow.

The streets were ours and we were going to make it known to all the other gangs. I can recall one Friday when we went to a concert at a school, I was having a lot of fun with my girlfriend when the unexpected happened – war broke out with a rival gang. It escalated so fast that all I could hear was screaming. Blood was being spilt and patrons were running and screaming for the police because of what they were now witnessing first-hand.

The injuries were grave and many. That night I ran until I threw up on myself. I was stabbed in my side but somehow there was no blood coming from the wound. I was only sixteen at the time it happened and I felt like I was going to die that day. This event took such a mental toll on me that I can't tell how I got wounded in the mayhem. I subsequently spent three months in the hospital but had no remorse for the damage that I inflicted upon innocent people. All I wanted was blood; I was going to make them pay for what they did to me and the severe pain they caused. The pain I experienced and the nasty scar that was left in my abdomen, filled me with rage and I only wanted to do harm to people.

A few months went by without any incidents because I was recovering from my injuries. One Sunday morning all the leaders from the "Money Gang" decided to go to the beach with us. This beach was one of our favorite spots, as it was frequented by tourists who had many valuables. On our way to the beach, we encountered five members of a rival gang. This was the first time that I injured someone and felt sorry that I did it. This guy was old enough to be my father, but I was armed with a very sharp dagger, and I decided to use it. The fight was fierce and a few of the guys were badly injured. I still remember the look of fear in that man's eyes after her got injured. My notoriety started spreading and everyone knew my name and how fearless I was. I started attracting women that were even older than I was; some were close to my mother's age.

My heart was becoming more hardened towards people, and I was one of the worst on my block. My crimes were at a different level, and I was getting more respect on the street – or so I thought. I was a brutal and heartless young gangster who didn't care about people's feelings anymore.

Smoking Cannabis or Ganja as we call it in Jamaica, drinking alcohol and sexual exploits made me feel like I was a grown man. I

4

eventually became involved with prostitutes, both sexually and commercially, selling their bodies and paying me a protection fee. My friends and I would go on the street at nights to rob people who were lured by the prostitutes. It was easy and I loved it because my girls would always call me to give me the drop on guys who showed up with a lot of cash to spend. This was what we knew and the hustling in the street at night meant survival and a source of income.

The gang I was a member of now numbered in the twenties and with the strength in our number, we easily secured turf. We were a legion of hardened gangsters, and everyone knew about and feared us. We preyed on the weak and vulnerable, including school children and would take on any other gang who attempted to do what we did. My closest ally in the gang had a passion for hurting people and I enjoyed going out with him because I knew we were unstoppable together. He was like an enforcer in the gang who had no qualms being brutal to other guys.

I was only seventeen years old, and my life was getting tougher each day as I was getting a lot of heat from other gangsters and the police were now searching for us in relation to a shooting incident in our community. I feared for my family's safety because the feud that I became involved in was escalating in my community and people were getting hurt. I was on the brink of losing my life. Gangsters and police alike were searching all over for me. It was only then that I started thinking of my family and the problems that I brought, especially to my mother's doorstep. The police were going to my mother's house looking for me, and gangsters were everywhere in the street searching too.

We had a lot of influence as young gangsters, reckless and carefree, disregarding God, laws, and men. Man, I was loving my gangster life! I had the ambition to grow up to become Jamaica's "Scarface" like in the movies – ruthless, heartless, and showing no sympathy to anyone. The respect I got became addictive and I loved it. Through fearmongering, I got whatever I needed from people. The older men were giving us anything we needed out of fear for what we might do to them. If they didn't comply with our orders, we would make their lives quite uncomfortable in unconscionable ways. In my mind I was like a god who did anything I wanted at my own pleasure and took from people as I pleased.

Elders of our community who owned grocery stores had to fulfill our grocery orders and put it on our tab, which was never paid. They complied to ensure that their children, wives, or relatives were being taken care of on the street.

While I was playing the antagonist and making in-roads as a young gangster, trouble was never far from me. It followed me wherever I went like a shadow. One day while waiting on some friends in town, I was attacked and stabbed in my abdomen. This injury was so serious that I had to be admitted in the hospital for two months. While in recovery and undergoing treatment at the Cornwall Regional Hospital, someone gave me up to the police. Upon their investigation, they found me laying in the hospital bed with IVs attached to me. They proceeded to secure me to the bed with a handcuff, and as soon as I was discharged from the hospital, I was arrested and taken to the Barnett Street Jail.

CHAPTER 2
Tribulation

———

In 2016, GOD in His mercy, took me up from a woman's bed, thwarted my sexual exploits and took me to a tent crusade where He started me on a new journey. I made the choice to take the plunge into the watery grave of baptism that very night and bore witness to the world that I desired change. I felt all my burdens leave me, but only for a short time in my life. I guess I was looking for some spiritual immunity from the reality of life. I thought to myself that now that I'm a follower of Christ, all my troubles would vanish. This couldn't be farther from the truth.

The day following my baptism, I was at home pondering my case that I had in court. I was troubled by what the possible outcome might be. I was a gangster before I give my life to Christ Jesus; no one dared to disrespect me or pick a fight. I was short-tempered, hot-headed and ruthless. The case I had in court pertained to an illegal firearm and the prosecutors wanted to show the public that I was a fake and that I got baptized only in an effort to elude justice, judgement and prison.

My tribulation was now more than I could really manage; the possibility of going to prison was right there at my door step. Here I was again with my back against the wall. This was the second time I was charged with breaking the law. My life looked bleak as a new born Christian, but I remained optimistic all the way. I accepted Christ and His word even when people rejected me, because God's word gave me the assurance that I needed in Matthew 21:42 – "Jesus said unto them did ye never read in the scripture. The stone which the builder rejected, the same is become the head of the corner?"

Following the trial, it became mandatory for me to report to the police station three times weekly; this was done to ensure that I remained in Jamaica. Early one morning I reported to the police station and the officer who caught me with the illegal firearm was on duty at the front desk. When I saw him, my heart sank, and I felt a sharp pain in my chest. Many youngsters who become involved in crime and get caught, are treated harshly by some officers and are constantly on the police's radar. This is an extremely uncomfortable feeling, take it from me; but in that moment, God gave me assurance from His holy word in Lamentations 3:22-23 – "It is of the Lord's mercies that we are not consumed, because his compassions fail not. They are new every morning; great is thy faithfulness."

I was subsequently slapped with a severe prison sentence by the judge to do four years, hard labor, in prison for the illegal possession of a firearm. While the sentence was being handed down, my lawyer stood silent, looking at me without a single appeal to the judge on my behalf. I was terribly angry at him, and everyone involved in my case; this was too much for me at this time. I lamented the fact that so many years of my life were to be spent in a prison system built to oppress, but there was no one to blame but myself.

It was foolish of me to get involved in something of which I already knew the outcome would be disastrous. I could not cope with all the challenges and difficulties I was once more going to face in my life. I wasn't getting any younger and time waits on no man. I was sent back to prison again, only this time, in my own country. I knew it was going to be tough and you can't be soft in prison, because people will take advantage of you in any way they can.

I was sent to the prison in Spanish Town, St. Catherine to do my time. Upon my arrival, I saw a few guys that I knew from the streets, but in prison, rules and laws are different, trust is in short supply and you don't know anyone until you are sure they are with you. Even in this environment, you must be careful of the persons with whom you align yourself. If someone you know from the street is being targeted in prison and you affiliate yourself with such a person, you are sure to become a target as well.

My mother and aunt were not aware of the inner workings of being in prison, so they brought me a lot of food to take with me to prison since I would be out of parish and far away from family. Some of the officers on duty would confiscate your possessions and classify them as contraband even if they weren't, and there is nothing you can do about it. It's frightening and you must tread carefully as an inmate because you can go into prison and never make it back home if you don't make the right choices. Yes, even in prison, making the right choice is critical to your survival. The trials were real, and your life could easily become a living hell if you were not careful.

In prison, there were inmates who were also wardens. They are the ones who give instructions and schedule time for meals, showers, and yard breaks. The first chore of the day is typically to dispose of your waste which was excreted in a jug or bottle that you used during the night, because there are no toilets inside the cells for this purpose. It is crucial that you pay close attention to your personal receptacle and ensure it doesn't come into contact with another inmate – this mishap can get you killed.

Another thing that can get you killed while behind bars is referring to another inmate as a "boy". This is seen as very disrespectful as this label is reserved for those who have homosexual tendencies and are marginalized. Even in this environment, proper use of language and vocabulary is important.

Prison is a 'kill or be killed' environment where it is difficult to avoid trouble. Sometimes you have no choice but to deal with situations like a man and bite the bullet as the tribulation and temptation you encounter daily, backs you into a corner. There are inmates who are referred to as "trouble makers" – seemingly notorious and untouchable fellows. Sometimes they are serving life sentences or an excessive number of years, so they don't care if they live or die. While the objective of incarceration may be to reform you and help you become a better person, life in prison can make you become pernicious as a result of the conditions and treatment inflicted by fellow inmates and guards alike.

The death of my little brother at the hand of a gunman in my community, broke my heart and brought me to the realization of how poisonous I was in all my doings. I was so perplexed by his death that I often thought of exacting street justice for the cruel act that was carried out on my little brother, but that would only put me back into that dreaded box or get me killed, finally. The pain is hard to bear, especially when you get word of who the perpetrators may be and know how to find them. A life of crime has no rest, inside or out. I guess it was a taste of what I too, once did.

CHAPTER 3

Incarcerated

———

After being imprisoned for about three months, I saw my best friend brought into jail and shortly after, my other partner in crime was with us. We were all in jail facing charges of shooting with intent. When we appeared in court, the judge ordered us to be remanded in custody at the Spanish Town prison for three months before our official hearing. At our arraignment the judge granted us bail in the sum of fifty thousand dollars per person. Luckily, my mother was there to bail me out. Two of the three of us were released that day.

Now that we were out, one of my friends turned on me and started telling my mother that I was the troublemaker. When I heard this from my mother it made me furious to know that my best friend betrayed me, so I no longer respected him. We continued going to court for the shooting case but by the mercy of God I was the first one that was freed from the charges, followed by this friend. My other partner was unfortunately slapped with a twenty-year prison sentence with hard labor. He was killed by poisoning after serving five years of his sentence.

As it turned out, my other friend who betrayed me joined a rival gang but I wasn't abandoned, I had other friends now. I was now a part of a gang of five. My name changed from "Money" to "MOB" and I was with guys who were handling real money and who had a lot more influence and respect.

Red was like my big brother and looked out for me. He gave me cars to drive, put money in my pocket, bought me clothing and took me wherever he went. The money and being in the company of Red didn't make my life easier. I was in the crosshairs of my old friends who were now in another gang. A new feud developed and things got so hot that guns came into play and we were going at it in broad day light. This put a new target on my back and the police was again searching for me as a person of interest in the matter.

I decided to take revenge on my rivals and used their girlfriends to get us the information we needed such as their whereabouts and plans. The gang feuds quickly became very heated and hitmen were brought in from elsewhere to get rid of us. As soon as we got wind of the plot to take us out, and knowing the police were also on our trail, the top men in the gang funded our migration and we all ran away to the Bahamas and eventually to Miami, Florida.

Upon reaching Miami we were picked up by border patrol and put in a Federal Detention Centre by ICE while waiting to see a judge to decide our fate. We were eventually released with an ID card and a temporary social security number that was good for six months while we awaited a decision on whether we would be deported back to Jamaica. Life started looking fruitful for all of us; we were in another country where things were much easier for us.

I was now twenty years old and ready for whatever came my way. My family needed help and I got the chance to make a choice to change it and I was going to make it my duty to take care of my mother and grandmother back home in Jamaica. I was happy for the chance because I brought so much pain upon my family and had my mother going back and forth to the jail house and paying medical bills for persons I hurt.

Kip was a mafia of sorts and I considered him my brother from another mother. The love and respect we had for each was so strong that people would think we were biological brothers, and we didn't make them any wiser. When we first arrived in Tampa, Florida we all stayed together in one apartment, forming our own support system.

There was a girl whom I met a few years before who was living in a nearby town. She was a nurse and would do anything to make me happy. She was so beautiful inside-out. There are no words deep enough or sweet enough or fine enough that can explain her beauty. She was so nice to me that I took her kindness for weakness, and I started treating her badly. As the problems worsened so did the stress level. Life wasn't going well for us in Florida so Red took Kip and I up to Washington DC, but nothing was working in our favor there either. Kip and I decided to move back to Florida to make something happen.

I stayed with Red in Orlando for a while where he taught me the code of the street life there. After some time passed, I decided to return to Tampa to live with some other friends. Life was hard for us because we didn't have jobs or money to sustain us and cover our rent. Pressed for resources, we set our sights on peddling drugs and started finding people who could get us into that game.

Kip met a girl who knew all the "dope boys" in the neighborhood and she would let us know all the dealers in the street. I finally got in and started hustling and making a few dollars. I quickly learned how to turn a profit and increased my intake. There was no turning back now. My life was joyful now and I could afford to buy a real bed and throw out the air mattress I had. I was on the rise and my future looked good, in my mind. I started attracting all kinds of girls – Latina, white and black - I was living out my dreams in the United States of America.

My friends and I were good now; we were known as 'the dreads on the block'. Some people started disliking us due to our success, including some of our elders who had put money together to take us from Jamaica. They were concerned that we were moving too fast, but I was about my money, no games, no jokes. We were very serious about securing "the cheddar" and would defend it at all costs.

As I went about my business, I met Mel who lived two blocks away from me. I was messing around with another girl at the time but there was something about Mel that I loved beyond sex. She was a real hustler who knew the street code of the game. She was as serious as I was about money and she let the other guys know that her man was a crazy Jamaican who enjoyed hurting people, especially those who messed with his money.

Worldly things were taking over my life. I want a big house, cars and the latest clothing, jewelry and lots of money. Nothing was going to stop me from achieving my goals even if I had to take a life, that's how determined I was. I needed money to send back to my mother in Jamaica plus money to take care of my women and pay the bills.

Things were going great for us for a while until the authorities caught up with Red. When he was arrested and put in jail, it cut off my connections and took me right back where I started. My financial resources started drying up and life started getting hard again. I got into an altercation with a colleague who had wrongfully accused me, but he got the best of me since he was a bigger guy. I was not about to be disrespected and I made it known, loud and clear. I got access to a gun and fired at him, but he wasn't injured. This reckless action caused a warrant to be issued for my arrest for shooting with intent.

The sheriff received all the necessary information they needed to find me, but I found a quiet place to stay low for a while. My hustling was now on hold because I couldn't touch the street because the sheriff was looking all over for me. It took me almost three months before I started hustling again.

My life was a complete mess now and I was angry with the world. I had insidious and pernicious thoughts that led me to start robbing people, all in an effort to get back into the game.

I was working very hard so that I could assist my family in Jamaica plus my women and Kip, who was caught by the authorities and deported to Jamaica. Although I was involved in wrongdoing, there was one girl who cared for me and wanted me off the street. She worked extra hours to earn enough to take care of me, but despite her concern, efforts, and hard work, I wasn't about to quit this game.

CHAPTER 4

No Quitting the Game

———

Quitting my hustle was the farthest thing from my mind as I started seeing the benefits of it. It was all I knew and I didn't have the basic qualifications needed to find a normal job. I dropped out of school at a very tender age while I was in grade nine in junior high school. I was expelled due to my bad behavior and I turned to the street for solace and belonging. I would eventually get access to a gun and that made me want to kill anyone who tried to disrespect me, my family and friends.

In November 2000, my life was going to change for the worst in Tampa, Florida. It was a Thursday, and my plan was to spend the whole day and night with my family and take my girlfriend and her kids out to dinner. We went to the Red Lobster restaurant and had a fantastic time together. On our way home we stopped at the Block Buster store to get some movies to watch later that evening. We then went grocery shopping and headed home. Upon arrival we noticed a few of my friends were at the house awaiting my return, but my girlfriend wasn't pleased to see them at all because she knew they were trouble. Our romantic night together ended abruptly.

She knew they were up to no good and were only there to get me involved in their sinister plans. As she suspected, they were there to ask me for my assistance to carry out a robbery that they had planned. I was a little confused and hesitant at first because I really wanted to stay home with my family but another part of me wanted to help my friend get that money. They were my partners in crime and we pledged to support each other no matter what the situation was. We were always there for each other in times of need, so I took out a bottle of Hennessy and some cannabis, and we started drinking and smoking to prepare for our antics.

My woman must have been listening to our conversation, because she called me into the bed room and tried to dissuade me from leaving the house. I had promised her that I would spend the entire day and night with the family. Feeling the need to keep my word to my friends, I told her I was only leaving for twenty minutes, then I gave her a kiss and walked back to our living room where I took up my little Bible, placed it in my pocket, grabbed my car keys and headed out the door.

My friend got in touch with his contact, a very cunning woman who was playing both sides of the field. She set up all the robberies and would get a cut from the loot. On the flip side, if we got robbed by other gangs, she still got paid because she set up gigs for them too. It was high stakes gambling, but I was down for whatever my friend was doing.

Even if people were to die, I was in all the way. I had a killer instinct like they did and I was ready to die with them also. We were a group of young gangsters from Jamaica and feared by many. It was our way of life and we were ruthless in it and willing take down anyone who was not a part of our circle.

We headed to our destination in two different cars. When we arrived, we walked towards a shed at the backyard of a white guy's house, but when we entered the shed, I was very uncomfortable. I felt like a spirit from God came over me, telling me not to do the deal with these guys because it was a setup. I turned to my friend and advised him that we should leave this place because something wasn't right. We both turned and walked out, one behind the other.

Just as we stepped out, we observed a county Sheriff's car nearby and we narrowly escaped being detected. We then retreated to a corner store where we got ourselves cigarettes, beer, and some other items. Red was nowhere to be found though; he had left with my car, so I was unable to get home. I had a bad feeling about the robbery and for some reason God's Spirit touched my heart in that shed. God decided to step in, but I was so far away from Him that I really didn't care. I felt like I would kill to get our riches and I knew without a doubt that my friends felt the same. We were hardened and ready to do whatever it took to put money in our pockets.

CHAPTER 5
In the Face of Death

———

When you're hustling in the streets you often don't see trouble coming until it's right in front of you. The turning point happened in my life when we decided to make a second attempt at the same deal that God had rescued us from. The first time we tried, we met two white guys inside the shed where the deal should have taken place, but this time around there were three white guys waiting for us inside the shed. Again, I felt uncomfortable and told my friend we needed to go immediately. I exited the shed with my hands in my pocket – I was armed. One of the men followed me out with my friend closely behind him. It was intense.

I don't know what type of power took over my friend, but I heard him using some profane words before he turned around and returned to the shed. That's when all hell broke loose. All I heard was a barrage of gun shots. The first thing that came to my mind was that my friend was killing these men. I was then grabbed from behind, around my neck by this giant white guy, he was squeezing the life out of me. I had my hand in my pocket, gripping tightly to the gun, but scared to death to discharge it. I somehow managed to remove his giant hands from my neck while trying to keep the firearm secure.

I was praying for my friend to come to my aid and take control of the situation because this giant white guy was squeezing the life out of me. I thought about using the concealed weapon I had but I didn't; I just wanted to get free from this guy. I then felt something hit me square on my nose and I fell flat on my back – I was shot! That's when I decided to fire a bullet from the gun I had, in a desperate attempt to scare them off. While I was still down, one of the men started kicking me in my face, cursing and calling me a dumb nigga. Another man came over to where I was laying and shot me twice, one bullet to my face and the other in shoulder. I then whispered a silent prayer to God saying, Lord it seems I came to the United States to throw my life away.

At this moment I saw a light, it was the brightest I've ever seen. I felt like I must have died. I was shot, bleeding and being beaten until I lost consciousness. When I regained consciousness, I found myself locked inside the shed. It was so dark that I couldn't even see my own hands. I managed to get to my feet, but I was bleeding badly from my nose and eye. I still had my cell phone, so I called my girlfriend, but I hung up before she could answer. I called another friend instead and told him what transpired, but he wanted nothing to do with this matter and abruptly ended the call.

I attempted to call my girlfriend again but the thought of the impact this would have on her caused me to hang up again.

I didn't know who else to call in that moment but a voice inside my head was telling me to call the police, and I did. A female officer answered the phone and asked how she could assist, and I told her that I have been shot in my face twice and I didn't want to die. I started crying when the officer asked me for my location, where I lived, who my parents were, and other questions. I kept repeating that I didn't want to die while crying. The officer told to me stay on the phone and to keep talking to her until help arrived. Shortly after I heard sirens blaring in the distance and coming in my direction while the officer continued to speak.

When the police arrived on the scene, they came to the shed, but the door was chained and locked with a padlock. The officer asked me if there was anyone else inside with me, but I was alone. He then instructed me to place my hands where he could see them, and that's when I informed him that I was shot in my face, twice. Writhing in pain, I put my hands in front my face and in seconds my palms were filled with my own blood. As I raised my hands above the top of the door, the police noticed the blood and raised an alarm. They tried getting the keys for the padlock, but they were nowhere in sight, so they resorted to cutting the chains off the door to get me out. The last thing I remember was the police screaming "freeze, hands on your head!", then I must have passed out because I don't recall what happened next.

The next day I woke up in the Tampa Bay General Hospital, waiting to be treated by a doctor. Standing beside my bed in tears, was my girlfriend. Oblivious to what had happened the night before, I asked her why she was crying and she replied, "you were shot". I looked at her and said, "you are crazy, I wasn't shot" and ignoring her advice, I attempted to move, only realize that I had IV tubes in my arm. I then inquired about my friend but received no answer as the doctor instructed her not to advise me about my friend's situation, because it could be traumatic and dangerous to my health at this time.

Two days later, a specialist came into my room with a drill and iron rods. Confused, I inquired about the purpose of the tools, and he looked at me and laughed; "they're for you", he said. The iron rods were to be placed inside my forehead to stabilize my neck to prevent the lodged bullet from moving. I was experiencing severe pain; however, my girlfriend was at my bedside providing support and consolation. She watched as the doctor marked my forehead at the points where he was going to drill holes to install the iron rods to stabilize my neck, not knowing what was coming next.

It was time for drilling to start and when the specialist got to work, I started screaming like a woman in childbirth. My girlfriend exited the room for she could not stand to watch me in so much pain; it broke her heart. Finally, the halo was placed around my head to stabilize my neck, and this was to stay in place for the next three months. It was going to be hard because these implements weighed about fifteen pounds. My girlfriend continued to be there for me throughout this ordeal and told me she thought of me as a noble warrior whom God saved for a purpose. She said she believed that God wanted me to do his will here on earth and that's the reason my life was spared. God has His ways of getting our attention when he needs it.

I didn't believe that it was time for me to do God's will because I was only twenty-one years old, just got shot and lost my best friend. I was determined to seek vengeance, then perhaps, do God's work. I was hurt and angry at the world and I hated all white people. I had no doubt that my friend would want me to seek revenge and was certain he would do the same for me.

Six months after I was shot, I was arrested and charged with first degree murder, aggravated felony with a deadly weapon, and delivery of cannabis. All those that I loved the most had turned their backs on me. All my friends were gone; there was no one to help me in my tribulation. Five months later, my murder charge was changed to murder in the second degree, a lesser charge, but it was easier to convict me since they didn't have to prove beyond a reasonable doubt, that I was guilty of this crime.

You see, the murder I was charged for was that of my best friend, whom I never killed, but they charged me for his death anyway, and that hurt my heart daily. I cried day and night for him, we were like brothers, and we did everything together. I was very sorrowful, especially when I saw his mother trying to send me to prison for her son's death. She had a personal vendetta against me for the death of her son.

After being released on bail, I realized that no one was going to help me get back on the street. I was angry at everyone, and my heart became ice cold. I cared nothing about people's feelings anymore. "I was going to prison, and no one cared, so why should I care about people's feelings?", I asked myself. My heartbeat that I loved so much, also left me at a time when I needed her most.

The whole judicial system was against me and there was no way I was going to beat this case with all the evidence that was mounting up. I eventually accepted a plea deal from the State of Florida for fifteen years on second degree felony murder; fifteen years for aggravated felony with a deadly weapon, and five years for delivery of cannabis. I was sentenced to thirty-five years imprisonment, running concurrently, meaning I would serve a total of fifteen years in prison, and I was only twenty-one years old at the time. I desperately needed support from my sweetheart and family, but there was no one to depend on.

I was first taken to the Orient Road Jail of Hillsborough County then was transferred to the Jackson County Apalachee Correctional Institution to carry out my sentence. My first day in prison was like hell. I was young and didn't know what life was like in prison. Owing to my age and inexperience, the inmates I was housed with stole my clothing and food, and there was nothing I could do about it. My cellmate, who was doing a life sentence, had questionable tendencies and he would set up his friends to steal my belongings at mealtime when I left the cell. The thought of ending his life while he slept, was very tempting.

I became their new target and they continued to prey on and steal from me. I was so hurt and upset but had no friends to come to my aid, nor could I go to the guards about my situation because I would be labeled a snitch. In prison, no one likes a snitch, not even the guards. I was a young and vulnerable prisoner, so I decided to make a name for myself like others did. I was going to be locked up here for fifteen years and I had neither girlfriend to come and see me nor did I have my family. I was alone in a foreign country, heartbroken because I let down my mother, grandmother, and the rest of my family.

After my orientation was complete, I was assigned to a kitchen job which shockingly only lasted for one day. Why? I attempted to take food from the service line only to be told that I wasn't allowed to eat anything from the line until the entire compound was fed. This made me angry, so I decided not to return to the kitchen for duty, not knowing what consequences would follow.

The officer in charge of the kitchen had me locked up for refusing to work and I was subsequently isolated for sixty-eight days in the box as punishment. After my time in the box was over, I was re-assigned to another job, one which was harder than the one before – it was outside. This meant that I would have to work in the hot sun, cutting grass from nine in the morning to three-thirty in the afternoon. I had no intention of continuing to do this job, so I used my blood pressure illness to fake a fainting episode. The officer that oversaw my unit took me to the clinic to see the doctor, who wrote me a medical pass to stay out of the sun.

I was eventually re-assigned to a different dormitory where I met some inmates from the Virgin Islands who were doing life sentences for murder and various other crimes. I told them about my roommate and what he did to me. I formed an alliance with the men from the Virgin Islands and they were willing to kill for me because of how I carried myself in prison; I was very militant and always minded my own business and fought for whatever I believed in. I was a really "stand-up" guy who was willing to die for my rights at all costs.

With my reassignment came new duties to work in the laundry room. I liked this job because I got the chance to hustle a little money to maintain my needs in prison. There was a Muslim man who also worked in the laundry but assigned to the shoes room whom we all called "Mike Tyson" because he had a stark resemblance to the former heavyweight boxer. He was larger in stature than I was, so he figured he could bully me. Everything the other inmates did he blamed me for it and slandered my name. Early one morning I found myself blaming God for everything that was happening to me in prison. This was when my quest for destruction started.

The Muslim man approached me inquiring about some shoes he had packed in a box for disposal, the contents of which was now all over the floor in his working quarters. He started accusing me of doing it even when I told him it wasn't me, but he wouldn't listen. In my frustration and anger, I told him every disrespectful word I could find and was ready to fight because I didn't fear him nor anyone else for that matter. This got him really worked up to the point where he punched me in the back of my neck when I wasn't looking. I was hit so hard that it felt like the lodged bullet had moved in my neck. I was unable to move my neck for a couple of minutes and the pain was excruciating. I told him that he was a dead man walking especially because I was innocent of his accusations.

Another Jamaican man who had been incarcerated for over thirty years, gave me a knife to defend myself against this man. I was determined to retaliate but I could not get to him inside the laundry room, so I had to fight him like a man, bare-fisted. The first punch I landed knocked him over on his back and I started kicking him while he was on the ground. Some of the other inmates had to pull me off him. He became the laughingstock, but this was far from over. He told his Muslim brothers about our incident and when I returned to my dormitory quarters where we both lived, he was there waiting to start round two.

He wanted to fight me again, but my cellmate told me not to worry and reassured me that no harm would come to me. He was ready to come to my defense and even kill because he was already serving a life sentence and had nothing to lose. These men knew what would happen if a brawl occurred, so one of them came over to speak with me and apologized for what had transpired earlier that day inside the laundry room. The conflict ended, but I still watched his every move until I was transferred to another institution for wounding another inmate.

The devil really had me where he wanted because at this new prison, I was doing things I had never done in my life. I was sexually inappropriate with the female staff and even masturbated in front of them. I acted without care and was not concerned about the consequences I would suffer. I got a level of satisfaction from disrespecting the female staff. I disrespected every guard and rebelled against the treatment I received, but every time I did this, I was placed in solitary confinement. All my personal effects were confiscated and distributed to other inmates of the prison as punishment for my actions.

Despite this, I became even more rebellious and heartless towards the officers and prisoners alike. Proverbs 14:12 says "there is a way that seems right to a man, but the end thereof is the way of death". I was severely punished and was physically abused by guards for my actions. This compelled me to cry out to God, who, at the time, I didn't even know or believe in.

God knew my every thought; He knew why I was doing all these things and He knew that at some point I would turn away from my sins and glorify His holy name. He saw my future and knew that I would come to proclaim that Jesus Christ is the son of the true and living God. He was only preparing me to carry out His work that I was assigned when the right time came. The Holy Spirit led me to this scripture in John 14:6 - Christ said I am the way, the truth, and the life which opened my understanding of the holiness and righteousness of the Creator of this vast universe. He was teaching me the things I needed to know about Him so that I would be effective when the time came.

CHAPTER 6
My Transformation

————

All my thoughts started changing and my life started to be transformed from darkness to light when the Holy Spirit guided me to Acts 4:12 which says – "Neither is there salvation in any other: for there is no other name under heaven given among men, whereby we must be saved." I started reading my Bible more, but I was still fulfilling the desires of my flesh; I was still behaving inappropriately in front of the nurses, doctors, and other female guards. Whenever I was being placed into solitary confinement for my actions, I would act crazy so that they would take me back to the clinic where all the female staff were. When it was time for me to see the psychologist, I put feces all over my body and face which forced them to classify me as insane and refer me to a psychiatrist for mental health treatment.

I was placed on all types of medication which I refused to take because I knew nothing was wrong with me. The fact that a bullet was lodged in my head caused the doctor to think that I was affected by it, which was exactly what I wanted to hear to justify my actions. I knew I was not crazy, but when I reflect on it, I really must have had some form of mental illness to do some of the things I did.

My actions were of the devil, but my heart's desire was to please God. My flesh was weakened by a life of sin but the Holy Spirit, who is my comforter would to guide me to the scripture in 1 John 1: 6-7 – "If we say we have fellowship with him and walk in darkness, we lie, and do not practice the truth, but if we walk in the light as he is in the light, we have fellowship with one another, and the blood of Jesus Christ cleanses us from all sin." This Bible verse convicted my heart because I knew my actions were not right before God. It made me cry like a newborn baby, my heart's desire was to truly do the will of God and submit all my ways to his righteousness.

I was voracious for righteousness, so I continued reading God's word and the more I sought, the more I realized that God loved me, because the comforter was with me all the way on my quest. The next scripture The Spirit led me to was 2 Peter 3:9 – "The Lord is not slack concerning his promise as some count slackness, but is longsuffering towards us, not willing that any should perish but that all should come to repentance." I laughed to myself when I read all these Bible verses because I knew that I had hurt a lot of people in my lifetime. I was a savage young man who did bad things to people, so I felt like my soul was heading to hell, but God my Creator was telling me in His word that He's not slack concerning his promise, as some count slackness, but is longsuffering towards us.

I was going through turmoil at this time in my life. My best friend had just died, I was shot multiple times and now I was in prison. My mother and family were thousands of miles away and my father had recently passed away. Bombarded by all these thoughts, these words were constantly ringing in my head - CHOICE, CHANCE, CHANGE. I was rebellious and needed blood for what I was going through. I didn't really know what to do to bring back a little light into my heart. I didn't know how to pray or read well, but here I was reading and understanding God's holy word.

2 Peter 3:9 just kept playing inside my head, "the Lord is not willing that any should perish but that all should come to repentance." So, all I needed was to repent of my sins and all my troubles would go away? I asked myself. No one cared about me, all my friends abandoned me; my girl was gone, my best friend and my dad died, I was locked inside a prison cell being abused by these prison guards and here in the Holy Bible, God was telling me that he loved me - a sinner who broke every one of His laws.

When my mother and my father forsake me, then the Lord will take me up! The Lord took me up in my despair; when I thought I was alone the Lord was there with me all the way, but I was ignoring him to fulfill the lust of the flesh. Human beings tend to love sin. I was in love with smoking weed and drinking alcohol, I enjoyed sexual indulgence - it was my sweetest joy, and I wasn't married.

I enjoyed gambling and lying too. I was a liar and the Bible says that the devil is a liar, but holy and righteous is the name of God Almighty. I came to the point where I no longer found joy in doing these things because my heart was becoming fond of Jesus Christ, and the Holy Spirit was deeply impressing my dying soul. God was showing me in His word how much He loved me.

Exodus 23:25 says "And you shall serve the Lord your God, and He shall bless your bread and your water, and He will take sickness away from among you." I was amazed by all the wisdom and understanding the Holy Spirit gave me about Jesus Christ. "If you diligently heed the voice of the Lord your God and do what is right in His sight, give ear to His commandments and keep all His statutes, I will put none of the diseases on you which I have brought on the Egyptians. For I am the Lord who heals you." (Exodus 15:26). God was showing me that He is always in control of our lives. If only we would accept Him as the only true God.

Remember, I was acting crazy and doing things that only a person with true mental health issues would do. I was troubled with high blood pressure caused by stress from being forsaken by the people that I loved the most. God wanted to heal all my diseases. Psalms 103:3 reminds us that it is God "Who forgives all your iniquities, and heals all your diseases." The word of God was telling me that only God could heal all my iniquities and cleanse me from all my sins. He was my doctor in the hospital, my lawyer in the court room, my friend in the time of trouble, He was a canopy over my head through the storm. Hallelujah! Someone should praise Him! I was deeply transformed by the wisdom and knowledge of God.

1 Corinthians 6:20 says "For ye are bought with a price; Therefore, glorify God in your body, and in your spirit, which are God's." God was showing me that I was bought with a price by the blood of his only begotten son, Jesus Christ. Galatians 3:13 reminds us that "Christ has redeemed us from the curse of the law, having become a curse for us (for it is written, "Cursed is everyone who hangs on a tree"." Hebrews 9:12 says "Not with the blood of goats and calves, but with His own blood He entered the Most Holy Place once for all, having obtained eternal redemption." These are the words of God that were speaking to me about Jesus Christ and showing me that my God is awesome, He is holy, He healed me when I was broken, strengthened me in my weakness - my God is awesome! He is the Savior of the whole world, by His stripes we

were healed. He is great and awesome; someone should testify of His holy name! He is my provider, and He can move mountains.

1 Peter 1:18-19 says, "Knowing that you were not redeemed with corruptible things, like silver or gold, from your aimless conduct received by tradition from your fathers, but with the precious blood of Christ, as of a lamb without blemish and without spot." These are the holy words that the Holy Spirit revealed to me about Jesus Christ and His lovingkindness towards sinners. God was now showing me the dark side which is sin and the penalty for transgression of His holy laws. Romans 6:23 tells us that "the wages of sin is death, but the gift of God is eternal life in Christ Jesus our Lord."

"Therefore, just as through one man sin entered the world, and death through sin, and thus death spread to all men, because all sinned." (Romans 5:12). "For if we sin willfully after we have received the knowledge of the truth, there no longer remains a sacrifice for sins, but a certain fearful expectation of judgment, and fiery indignation which will devour the adversaries. Anyone who has rejected Moses' law dies without mercy on the testimony of two or three witnesses. Of how much worse punishment, do you suppose, will he be thought worthy who has trampled the Son of God underfoot, counted the blood of the covenant by which he was sanctified a common thing, and insulted the Spirit of grace?" (Hebrew 10:26-29). The Holy Spirit was building me up through the knowledge of God. I felt so remorseful for the sinful things that I did; my heart was contrite, and I desired to do things that would please God.

How could I, a sinner, deserve spiritual death? I cried out my heart to the Lord and asked him to forgive me, a sinner, for my sins. The spirit led me to Numbers 14:18-20 – "The Lord is longsuffering and abundant in mercy, forgiving iniquity and transgression; but He by no means clears the guilty, 'visiting the iniquity of the fathers on the children to the third and fourth generation.' Pardon the iniquity of this people, I pray, according to the greatness of Your mercy, just as You have forgiven this people, from Egypt even until now." Then the Lord said: "I have pardoned, according to your word".

CHAPTER 7
Finding Purpose

I have never been baptized, but inside my heart and soul I really wanted to know if there was really a God, a supernatural being that created everything. I continued doing things that were contrary to God's holy laws. I was still lustful but I remembered that the Bible stated that I can't serve two masters at the same time, because you will love one and hate the other.

Deep down inside my soul I knew that God was preparing me for a great cause, a duty in His name, and yet I refused to be obedient to His holy words. I lied, stole, created mischief, drank alcohol, smoked tobacco, cigarette and marijuana; but in my disobedience to God, He still saved and protected when I needed it most. I recall one morning when I was at a prison in Florida, we were on the recreation field playing soccer, when one of the most insidious things happened. There was an inmate, American by birth, but both parents were from Jamaica. During the match, this inmate kicked me on my ankle, sending pain all the way to my brain.

I asked him why he was playing that way and he hissed his teeth and walked away without answering. I had the sudden urge to punch him in the face, but I was waiting on the right moment to do it and the right time to beat the skin off his face. The same inmate kicked my cousin on his ankle also. My cousin was vexed and used a few profane words against him. He in turn responded with profane words and called both of us homosexuals and said we were sleeping with each other. I knew deep down that I was not gay, and his allegations grieved me to my core. When you are labeled as gay in prison and you don't stand up for yourself, you lose all respect from everyone.

I drew close to him until he was in my reach, punched him square in his mouth and we started fighting. On the recreation field there were two female guards on duty that day who noticed the fight, but turned away their faces as though nothing was happening. There were many Jamaicans on the recreational field playing dominos under a tree. I was of the devil, I feared no man and at that time, all I needed was blood. He went on to threaten me and warned me that I better have my knife with me when I came to the canteen for supper. Little did he know that we had knives buried everywhere around the soccer field.

I went and dug up a knife and placed it in my knee brace that I was wearing at the time. I strutted over to where he was standing with some others, with the intention of wounding him, but as I approached, he ran towards me and started throwing punches. I managed to dodge his punches and grabbed his shirt, pulling him close enough to injure him. I inflicted a few wounds before letting him go. He then ran to notify the guards of what happened and that he had been wounded by me and needed to see a doctor.

On his way to the clinic, he collapsed and this triggered a shutdown of the recreational field and the guards started searching for me. God was on my side because this inmate didn't identify me clearly. He reported that he was injured by a 'dread', so an investigation was launched into all the Jamaican inmates in an attempt to find out who the perpetrator was. We were all under lockdown for over six months before they transferred us to different prisons. I was the last one that was transferred to a prison built for rejected prisoners who weren't behaving themselves. This prison was referred to as 'closed management custody' and was filled with gangsters of all types.

My first day was like hell here because the guards didn't care about our wellbeing at all, and did things which they knew would have a mental effect on us, such as removing all our clothing in front of other inmates and searching our body cavities. These things hurt me to the core of my soul, to see how dismal my life was in prison. I wanted to kill all the guards because I saw them as my biggest enemies in the prison.

After the first day passed, I tried getting back into a regular routine, so I started exercising daily. I also started reading a lot to strengthen my vocabulary. I studied words and their meanings so I would know how to use them in the right context. My experience in prison was really challenging and I found that I harbored a lot of resentment toward God and evil manifested itself before my eyes. Inmates often attempted to offend me but they would find out that I was not a pushover.

I didn't really give my life completely to Christ Jesus at this time, so I was about to let them have what they were looking for – evil; but the spirit of God wouldn't allow me to fall back into the evil where it was taking me from. The flesh wanted me to unleash pain and shed blood. I was conflicted, hurting someone was ever in my thoughts, while at the same time I still wanted to do the things of God, because I felt a greater need for righteousness than sin.

Sitting down inside my cell, staring through the bars on a clear, starry night, I looked as far as my eyes could see and observed the hand of God, who made the stars, moon and other things. I felt the urge to jump and shout hallelujah and give God the praise and yet my heart wanted to kill people at times. Who could this be? I kept on asking myself. I knew that if God planted a seed inside me, no one could prevent it from springing up, not even myself at this point. I was being prepared to face the real world and the people that were in need of the good news of the gospel of Christ. I was the perfect vessel to bring this good news to the lost youth in the street. My life, image, and speech were all about the streets, because I was the street.

The streets helped to shape the man I grew to become - evil, ruthless and heartless. I was a young man who was kicked out of school at a tender age and void of knowledge. This made me really ignorant because everything seemed right in my eyes until someone proved me wrong.

The Bible teaches us about the lack of knowledge and the outcome of it. "My people are destroyed for lack of knowledge. Because you have rejected knowledge, I also will reject you from being priest for Me; Because you have forgotten the law of your God, I also will forget your children." (Hosea 4:6). I realized that because I lacked knowledge, I was doing the things of the devil who only wanted me to burn in hell.

"Then He will also say to those on the left hand, 'Depart from Me, you cursed, into the everlasting fire prepared for the devil and his angels." (Matthew 25:41). The fact that I was doing the things of the devil made me one of his servants. My mind was so poisoned that I became ruthless and heartless because of the tumultuous state of mind I was in. I wanted to hurt people for no reason. Satan who was my master, bid me to carry out his dirty work and dirty tricks. How could I resist the devil when I didn't even know Jesus Christ? I pondered. I recognized that sinners were really in need of Jesus Christ.

Sin really robbed me of my power from God. A quote from E.G. White states "Man was endowed with noble power and a well-balanced mind, he was perfect in his being and in harmony with God, his thoughts were pure, his aims holy, but through disobedience his power was perverted and selfishness took the place of love." "Our nature became so weakened through sin that it was impossible for us in our own strength to resist the power of evil. we were made captive by Satan and would remain so forever hadn't God specially interposed, it was the tempter's purpose to thwart the divine plan in God's creation in making man and fill the earth with woe and destruction, and Satan would point to all this evil he had done as the result of God's work in creating man".

I, being a natural man couldn't overcome Satan on my own. The Apostle Paul tells us in Ephesians 6:10-13 – "Finally, my brethren, be strong in the Lord and in the power of His might. Put on the whole armor of God, that you may be able to stand against the wiles of the devil. For we do not wrestle against flesh and blood, but against principalities, against powers, against the rulers of the darkness of this age, against spiritual hosts of wickedness in the heavenly places. Therefore, take up the whole armor of God, that you may be able to withstand in the evil day, and having done all, to stand."

I made the choice to take my stand for Jesus Christ and spread the good news of the gospel to weary and thirsty souls like mine. This was my purpose.

CHAPTER 8
Sobering Reflections

———

My worldly life was so sweet to me. How could I get over my sins without Jesus Christ? I loved smoking cannabis and I was very promiscuous. Selling drugs was my pride and joy because it gave me a lifestyle that no average man could afford. I was spending five to six hundred US dollars per night in the strip club. I felt so untouchable by the world as if I was a god; I did whatever pleased me. I was careless and my friends were all that mattered to me. We did whatever we wanted to anyone, anywhere, anytime, because we were fearless. We felt like top gangsters and we were making the laws in the street; we were in control. When I came to my senses, I realized that my life without God was real hell.

My time in the state prison was coming to an end and I was being prepared to be sent back to Jamaica with no money in my pocket, one pair of pants, one shirt, one pair of shoes and nowhere to go. I still hadn't surrendered my life to Christ, so just picture what I was going through. I had nothing.

I felt ashamed to see that I just did fifteen years in prison in the United States of America, only to return to Jamaica with nothing. I had no place to lay my head. A relative had taken over my space and here I was, fully dependent on someone, the very situation that I so desperately attempted to escape. I could do nothing without permission or had to sneak around because it was someone else's space and bed. Returning from the United States gave the impression that I had my own things, at least to the girls that started coming around. Little did they know that I was broke, stripped of everything I ever owned in my life - money, jewelry, cars, you name it. I was mad at the world to see that I didn't have what I wanted and here I was back in Jamaica and penniless.

I observed that many of my younger relatives were earning getting their own money, buying cars, and building houses and it made me feel less of a man because I had nothing. The condition I saw my mother in made me cry. I was the eldest of four sons for her and should have made it my responsibility and duty to take care of her, instead, she was the one who was taking care of me in prison while overseas.

When I was deported to Jamaica, I visited one of my friends who was also deported. We sat down and talked a little about our lives, our experience in the United States and our current living situation and how we could change it. It was then that I decided to call my girlfriend in the U.S. to ask her to send me three thousand dollars to take care of some business. My real intention was to pay for passage back to the U.S. I had a stash of cash that I had left behind that she had access to and she assured me she would get the money I requested. However, she was delaying sending the money, so I continued to ask, until one day the excuses started. She told me that the money she had in the safety box was in her aunt's name and she died, and her next of kin who had access to the box was in China and would not return to the U.S. for the next five years. I was left in shock, but there was nothing I could do, so I decided to focus on how I was going to earn money.

To hatch the perfect plan, I was introduced to a police officer – yes, this law man was crooked and did questionable things. I was still in the world doing the things of the world. I wanted to make money and almost lost my life, but God's grace kept me alive. One of the plans that we were a part of involved stealing millions of dollars, but we suspected it was a set-up. This officer had done a few robberies before with another crew, but he claimed the money was never shared right and that this robbery needed it to happen fast because his bills were growing, he had huge debt and his paycheck was woefully inadequate.

My mind was so fixated on making money that I couldn't see the grave danger this crooked cop was putting us in. He took us on three robberies that he said was cake walk and we trusted him until we went on our first operation with him and recognized he could not be trusted. I had a feeling that he was attempting to use us then kill us after we committed the robbery. Satan blinded my judgment with the millions of dollars to gain.

He called me several times the night before the robbery took place, but I was curious about his credibility, so I told him we needed guns and ammunition for the robbery because I didn't have a gun of my own. He said it was okay, so he brought us what we asked for and everything was in place for the robbery. We were prepared to whatever we had to do to get that money bag even if it meant we had to take a life. We meant business. There were five of us, me being the oldest one in the crew. A deportee, fresh from prison, broke, and broken, I was about to break the vow I made to God in prison. The devil was playing me again and I couldn't see it because I was so desperately in need of money and it blinded my judgment. The devil knew that I loved the Lord, but still loved the things of the world, so he used my need and weakness for money to lure me into a deadly situation and tried to take my life, but God saved me yet again for His glory.

God knew that through me, many people would be saved and people would come to praise and worship His holy name. There were four getaway cars waiting and I called the officer to ask him why the vehicle carrying the money was so late to arrive. He quickly responded that we should hold our positions and hung up. That's the moment it dawned on me that we were actually set up. Just we were about to leave, a police vehicle with three officers pulled up and they ordered me to stop and come over to them. I had a bag with an illegal fire arm in it and I thought of using it, but if I had reached for that weapon, I would have surely been a dead man.

I knew that being caught with an illegal gun would have dire consequences - my life or a long prison sentence. I was just coming from prison in the United States after serving a fifteen-year sentence for murder, drugs and aggravated battery, and the thought of going back to prison scared me to death. Just thinking about all of this made me really want to use the gun and make my escape. The spirit of God wouldn't allow me to throw away my life foolishly, because I was to become a vessel to bring the good news of Christ Jesus to lost souls. The Lord protected me in that desolate moment, although I had sinned against Him and broken the laws of the land.

There was a penalty to be paid for my actions. Just as criminals must pay the penalty for their crime, so sinners must pay the penalty for their sins. I sinned against God by being disobedient to His word that keep me alive all this time. I had let down my guard and allowed Satan once again to mess up my life. The moment I took up that illegal fire arm, was when the devil set his plan in motion to end my life. When I turned my back on Jesus Christ, I opened the door for the devil to destroy me. You see, God had a plan for me, and he was going to use this situation to change my life forever, for the glory of Jesus Christ.

A conversion and new birth in Christ were in progress. Let me here emphasize the necessity of conversion - Christ said "Of a certainty, except a man be born of the water and of the spirit, he cannot enter the kingdom of heaven". Ironically, when I got caught with illegal fire arm, my life changed; it changed for the glory of my savior Jesus Christ. I knew right then that God had created me for a purpose on earth he was just preparing me for a greater cause which was to lead obstinate people back to Him.

Jehovah God was just teaching me that I was to face greater trials in my quest to follow The Lord. He was showing me that there was much about life to learn beyond personal problems, unfairness and hardship. God was teaching me that for all that is hurtful and unequal, there is beauty and balance. For moments of horror and violence, there are times of harmony and peace. As age-worn bodies succumb to pain and weakness, God gives us fortitude to overcome. He was teaching me that there was no other like Him; my faith was being tested day and night.

I was thrown into jail again for this crime. All manner of crazy thoughts went through my mind as I reflected on being deported to Jamaica and in less than a year, I was back in same situation because I was foolish. I didn't even know if the gun I had was used in other crimes such as murder. Were people killed with this weapon? I asked myself. I just couldn't imagine myself in prison again, especially for crimes I didn't commit.

I cried in my heart day and night while in jail, where I was for a little over a month before I had a hearing in court and received conditional bail. A stop order was placed on me, so I could not leave Jamaica and go to another country.

CHAPTER 9
Love and Crime

———

The girl I was with at the time told me one day, that I was the dumbest man she had ever been with in her whole life. Instead of focusing and helping my mom, I was getting myself into trouble. I couldn't handle this at the time, especially knowing that I had strong feelings for her. I expressed my love for her through poems that I wrote, telling her how I wanted to take her on a special date on my magic carpet out into space. I wrote to her about how we would go roller skating around Saturn, then sit on a bed of clouds and toss stars into the milky way, where I would propose the crescent moon to her as an engagement ring before making love to her on a bed of clouds.

She was older than I was, but I trusted her and enjoyed her company so much that I could tell her anything as a lover and friend. She knew I had other girlfriends but she didn't make it an issue. This caused me respect her even more.

There was another girl who was my lover before I went overseas; it was love at first sight when I met her at the Old Hospital Park in Montego Bay. I had the opportunity to play a role in a movie at the time, but I was dangerous and actively involved in gang feuds. At the age of seventeen and feeling fearless, I started an affair with the director of the movie, but she was very untidy. I hated it so much that I became physically abusive. I missed rehearsals a few nights, and my girlfriend asked me if something was wrong why I was missing them. I told her what transpired, and she was completely shocked that I was having an affair with a grown woman at my age.

I knew my girlfriend liked my style because of the way she looked at me that night, but she spent a lot of time with three other guys and I wasn't sure which she was involved with. I was a gangster and didn't really care, so I moved in for the kill and invited her to a penthouse party and the rest was history. She was my person, my woman.

I enjoyed every moment we shared together but our communication was disrupted when I left Jamaica, and we broke up. After being deported, I ran into her again and it warmed by heart to see her; she looked better than ever, but my happiness was short-lived - she wasn't into me anymore. I was outraged by her lack of interest and I felt the urge to knock her out because I told myself that any woman that I had was mine for life. This was the gangster's way and it didn't matter if she was with someone else.

I was relentless in my pursuit and we eventually rekindled our romance for a while after, until she decided to tell me it was over. She was changing her life and wanted to serve God and leave the worldly things behind. This was the first time in my life that a woman decided it was over and I didn't put up a fight. We broke up but I felt nothing, because I had many other women fulfilling my sexual desires and others were in line awaiting their turn. I was still living the life I was attempting to leave behind. Most of my friends with whom I grew up in the street were now dead, but I was still here and was going to make known that I was back.

I met a new girl from Kingston, brown with clean, smooth skin. I really liked her, but she said I had too many women and she didn't want any trouble or drama in her life. I tried to convince her that I was single but she could tell I was lying and even knew the names of some of the other women. I couldn't believe my ears! How did she know all this? Who could be giving her all this information about me? I asked myself. I was determined to have her so I invited her to a party at a penthouse and she accepted. While there, she left my side for a moment to use the restroom, only to return to see me dancing with someone else. She angrily left the party that night and ignored me for months.

I still had a court date looming to answer charges for illegal possession of a fire arm. I was thinking of leaving Jamaica again because I didn't know what the outcome of my case was going to be. I didn't feel like returning to prison; who in their right mind would? I got word of a boat that was departing to the Bahamas but I needed to pay for passage. My friend told me that I could get onboard if I could procure twenty pounds of marijuana. Ten would be payment for the boat man and the remaining ten for me to sell upon arrival to put some money in my pocket. Although I was destined for the Bahamas, my eyes were fixed on returning to the United States.

When the time came for me to leave on the boat, I didn't have the required payment. However, I was the driver transporting the fuel for the boat; this was my bargaining chip. I had driven a diesel van that night and someone made a mistake and filled it with gas instead of diesel fuel. This threw a wrench into my plans as I had to take the van to a mechanic shop to have them sort it out. While I was taking care of this hiccup, the boat departed without me. I was scared sick because I would have to face the courts, but God didn't want me to leave Jamaica. A few days later, I got news that the boat was intercepted in Cuban waters with over three thousand pounds of marijuana on board. God prevented me from getting on that boat for a purpose.

My ex-girlfriend was going through a really hard time in her life at this point and wanted a change. She decided to reach out to me and apologize for the way she acted that night at the party; I accepted her apology and we reconciled. I took her on a few dates, this time with no sexual intentions, and this puzzled her because when we first met all I wanted was sex. I was in a different frame of mind, my case was weighing me down, so sex was the farthest thing from my mind.

I was required to report to the police three times per week and this was driving me crazy, only God knew the mental turmoil I was experiencing. The stress led me to smoking and drinking even more than I did before to take my mind off my problems. I would do anything to escape the impending judgement and neither drinking, smoking nor sex could ease my anxiety. All I knew was that I desperately needed a way out.

CHAPTER 10
When God Speaks

———

My girlfriend visited me one evening and I expressed my feelings to her and told her that I needed a 'release' later that night. She agreed, and told me to come to her house after she completed some errands. If you are a man that is in the world who drinks and smokes, when a woman decides to have sex with you, you know the protocol. You need to load up on liquor and weed. I did just that. I got rum and my weed and prepared for the night's events.

While preparing for my planned sexual encounter, the Spirit of God showed up and started instructing me. The voice said, "put down the weed", so I did. "Put away the liquor and put on your shoes", so I did. He then said, "leave the house", and I did. I stepped out and stopped a taxi without having a destination in mind. I boarded the cab and headed downtown. After driving for a few minutes, we came upon a large tent with a lot of people gathered there. I saw some lovely looking girls as well, and they drew my interest. I wasn't sure if seeing the girls made me stop, but the Spirit told me to get out of the car, and I did.

It was an evangelistic campaign that I was led to, and found myself walking all the way to the altar requesting baptism. I didn't know the pastor's name at the time, but in time I found that he was Pastor Charles Brevitt. It was a Wednesday night and the focus was on children, so he told me to come back on the following Sabbath to get baptized, which would have been the final day of the tent crusade. I told him that if I left without being baptized, anything I did would be on his shoulders. He then sent for Evangelist Shian O'Connor who agreed that I should be baptized. Coincidentally, my mother, my aunts and my girlfriend were all in the audience watching me get baptized. Perhaps being baptized on a night dedicated to children was symbolic of me becoming a child of God.

I wasn't fully aware of what I had done until I was on my way home and remembered that I had an appointment with my girlfriend that night. The reality then hit me, I just got baptized, but I still went to see her. What I did not know was, she was a former Christian and she was there when I got baptized a few hours before, so she said she would not commit fornication because I just got baptized moments before. The truth is, sex was far from my mind as well and I only went to see her because I had promised her to come over. She questioned the reason I made the decision to be baptized, if it was due to my impending gun charge. I told her I didn't know; I really didn't.

The timing was odd and I questioned myself too. We talked a little bit about God before I left and went home.

On the final day of the crusade, a Sabbath, a large crowd gathered. I heard the Evangelist ask the audience if they wanted the crusade to continue for one more week, and their response was a resounding YES. He asked them if they had nine hundred and forty thousand dollars for the expenses and the crowd went silent for a minute. This was the day that God was going to use me in a mighty way; in a way that He has never done before.

I gave a testimony about my life. I stood up for Jesus Christ and the heart of a rich person in the congregation was moved by my testimony. God inspired this person to donate a million dollars to the crusade to ensure that one more soul like mine could be saved. God continued using me in a mighty way. He placed some very influential people in my life, from ministers, doctors, and counselors to lawyers. It was a turning point in my life; God spoke and I responded.

CHAPTER 11
Facing Judgement

———

On the day of my sentencing, neither my mom nor any of the women I used to have a relationship with showed up. My impending judgement filled me with such terror that I turned to my Bible seeking some comfort but found none. I felt like God had turned his back on me, but He didn't. He sent me an angel to comfort me, in the form of Sister Brown, a lady who never left my side since the night I gave my life to the Lord. Here I was again in the court room, fighting for my life, not knowing what the judge was going to do. God already knew the outcome of my case and how long I would be behind bars.

I started reflecting on my first stint in prison in the United States and how I had to fight daily for my life. All those memories came flooding back, including the time I spent in lockdown for six years being confined to my cell for twenty-three hours daily, sometimes the whole twenty-four hours. I thought about how I might apply the few tricks I learned in the United States to the prison system in Jamaica, although I was almost sure that my experience here would be different. All types of crazy thoughts went through my mind at once. While sitting outside the court room on a bench, my probation officer came over where I was and give me a hug; this was alien to me. Never before has someone ever shown such compassion in my time of need. This lady was trying to comfort me by telling me everything was going to be well; that the judge would be lenient, and give me a fine or suspended sentence.

I was sweating profusely but the time was very cool. I walked out the building with the intention of leaving but turned back because I didn't want to get a bench warrant, which would only worsen my situation. Sister Brown could not come inside the court room, so she waited outside while I went in for my sentencing. There were a number of us with the same charge - illegal possession of a fire arm. Some were handed a twelve-month jail term, others, six months, then it was my turn. My name was the last one to be called and the judge told me to stand; my lawyer stood as well. I stood up and my charge was announced, for which I pled guilty. The judge then asked if I had anything to say for myself before my sentencing, to which I responded, "I am begging you for a chance sir". My response drew laughter from the judge and other persons inside the court room, then the judge's demeanor changed as he knocked the gavel and started reading my criminal history to the court.

He recounted that I was just deported from a state penitentiary in the U.S. for murder, drugs, and aggravated battery with a deadly weapon. His words caused my heart to sink, and I felt a heavy weight on my shoulders. I regretted not leaving when I had the chance while he read the letters of commendation which were submitted on my behalf from certain government entities such as the Peace Management Initiative (PMI), Citizen Security and Justice Program (CSJP), Pastors, and others. These letters proved that I was an evangelist and involved in church activities. He then said the most gut-wrenching words – "I sentence you to forty-eight months or four years of hard labor in prison". Tears filled my eyes as the reality of going back to prison hit me like a ton of bricks. My lawyer remained silent.

I was angry with God and with everyone else, especially those who were saying that I got baptized only because I was held with a gun. Some said I was not going to last longer than a week or a month at most. After I got my sentencing, I started thinking that maybe they were right. On my way out of the courtroom in chains, my lawyer told me that he would visit me, and I felt the urge to say unpleasant things to him, but the spirit of God tied my tongue. Sister Brown started crying when she saw me in chains but still managed to show me the love and support that I was in dire need of.

I was now on my way back to prison, this time in Jamaica, to do the time for my crime. My heart felt as cold as ice and hardened like concrete by the thought of going to prison. I thought of what I would do to anyone who tried to get in my way. All my life seemed to be behind bars as though I was a 'prison bird'. When would I get the time to find a wife and start my family? I asked myself. All my friends had a family, and I wanted a one too. Was I cursed?

I soon recognized that these were coming from the devil, he was trying to play on my mind again. What was surprising to me was the way the officers treated me this time around. It was different from my first experience behind bars. God was working, but I couldn't see it at the time because I wasn't focused on the things that He wanted me to do. The Bible reminds us in John 14:16 – "I will pray the Father, and He shall give you another Comforter, that He may abide with you forever".

There were four persons in the cell in which I was placed before I got there, I made it five. There was a lot of animosity between two of my cellmates who would get into frequent arguments which further heightened the tension inside the cell. I rekindled the habit of reading the Bible and to my surprise the words became life and were speaking directly to me. The same words that the Bible said, "came not in old time by the will of man: but holy men of God spoke as they were moved by the holy ghost" (2 Peter 1:21). "These are the things God has revealed to us by his Spirit. The Spirit searches all things, even the deep things of God" (1 Corinthians 2:10). These verses showed me that the Spirit of God was upon me, but I was not being humble for it to work on me effectively.

I started to pray and read more of the words of God, and that's when I noticed a change in my attitude towards the guards and inmates. Whenever I started reading, the whole cell became quiet, there was no distraction from anyone.

The female prisoners were asking me to pray for them in the mornings before court; the male prisoners were doing the same. When I prayed, everyone on the cell block would become quiet until I finished praying. Inmates sometimes asked that I read a Psalm for them before court and officers were asking me to say a prayer for their loved ones. Like Joseph, I found favor with the officers and was allowed to receive visits before my scheduled visiting day. Pastor Brevitt and Elder Greg visited me with gifts of books and food; they encouraged me as a new convert in prison. If only they knew the impact those books had on my life. I was deeply appreciative as I always enjoyed reading books that would uplift my spirit and educate me. I shared my food with my fellow cellmates as well as the word of God.

During the same week I was sentenced, I was transferred from the local jail to a larger correctional facility. I told the officers that I didn't have anything to bring with me to prison, but God was on my side. The officer took my mother's number, went straight to the desk, and made the phone call. The officer informed her that she could bring clothing, food, or money for me as fast as she could, seeing that the prisoner transportation was almost ready to leave. Soon after, I was summoned by the officer; my mother was outside to see me. I had the opportunity take a quick shower and have a little talk with my mother and aunt. They were both in tears as they encouraged me to be strong.

I don't know where I found the strength, but I was laughing so hard that my mother stopped crying. I jokingly told her that this was lunch time, and I would be out as soon as she returned home. My mother brought me a duffle bag with enough food that I was able to share with other inmates who were in need. Many of the convicts with a lesser sentence were worried sick about what would befall them in prison, some were first offenders, and marveled at my positive attitude. Owing to my previous experience, I was able to encourage them and give advice on how to handle themselves.

CHAPTER 12
Life on the Inside

———

Upon our arrival at the Spanish Town Correctional Institution, I recognized a few guys whom I knew from way back, who were serving time there too. However, with my experience I knew not to acknowledge them because I didn't know what they were in for or what activities they were involved in, especially sexually. In prison, it is important for you to know the behavior of your acquaintances for this will determine how you are treated by other inmates and guards. If your behavior is questionable, you were automatically sent you to what we called 'the boy's block'.

The guard brought us into the orientation room where we were searched for contrabands like phones, money, weed, cigarettes, etc. This is the part I hated with a passion because we had to take off all your clothing, squat, spread our gluteus maximus and cough really hard, while being closely observed by guards. This requirement diminished my integrity and moral value as it was very invasive, but this was a part of life on the inside. I wanted to cry at times, but this was my punishment for my crime. I had broken the law of the land again and I had to live with it until my sentence was finished. I often wondered about the guards and how they managed to carry out this task without being offended.

After we were processed and cleared, we were taken to a temporary holding area until our permanent holding was ready. New prisoners and juveniles were housed on Block A where they had one person to a cell. On the block for older men, there were three or five persons to a cell. I had two cellmates who were smokers but didn't have money to support their habit. They both knew I was a Christian, so they were hesitant to ask me for money.

One of the men who knew me before I was converted, came searching for me with marijuana, cigarettes and rolling paper; He didn't know exactly which cell I was in, so he was yelling my street name for this is what he knew. I responded and he proceeded to climb the bars and delivered the cargo to my cell. He then inquired about my whereabouts and old friends. I spent a few minutes recounting the events before he asked for what he really wanted, which was money and food. I gave him a few snacks and some money, and my roommates got the weed and cigarette they wanted.

I eventually pulled out the comforter I had received from my mother, spread it on the floor and fell asleep. I was later awakened by the biting of bed bugs, it was horrible. I was bitten numerous times all over my skin and was even bleeding. This nuisance kept me up all night as I desperately attempted to eradicate them.

I needed to empty my bladder in the wee hours of night, so I had to turn my water jug into a urinal. This was just one of the harsh realities of prison. I had to keep this receptacle close to me to ensure it didn't come into contact with anyone else. If your personal urinal were to mistakenly touch another man, that could be the end of your life. The following day I was paid a visit by another person I knew who asked about the happenings in our community. I didn't say much because I knew he was a "loose cannon" from the street, and I didn't really like him. I gave him some food from what I had; we talked a little longer, then he returned to his block. Prison is designed for people to use you for their own benefits, you don't really have friends in prison, because the day you don't have anything to give, is the day they want to kill you.

I also met a brother from another mother; we both came to prison at the same time and shared the same surname - Campbell. He was very knowledgeable and most persons underestimated him. At times when I had deep discussions about God with my cellmates, one in particular, would always make some solid points. I liked his energy, because great minds think the same, and I admired how he stayed focused on doing his time and going home to his family. I also developed great respect for my other cellmate who was very kind to me. He was the first person to give me a phone to call home and check in on my family. I was able to speak with my mom, brother, church sisters and brothers because of his kindness.

I also had the opportunity to contact a close friend of mine who was like a father to me. He treated me like his own son and would ask how I was holding up. We laughed about the situation as I would often joke that I was built for this. He would also see that my needs were met financially, as best as he could. I would ask him to send any money he had for me through my mother, because I trusted no one else.

This story would not be complete if I failed to mention Mrs. Heather Fray. This lady was always by my side from the moment I went to Salt Spring to make a presentation about crime and violence. She invited me to her church to talk with troubled youth about crime – something I ate for breakfast, lunch, and dinner in the past. This lady was there for me every step of the way while I was incarcerated. If I needed something that I couldn't afford, all I had to do was ask her. She offered spiritual counselling; if someone in my family was sick, she would see them, whatever I needed she was always there for me, even now. I am very much indebted to her, but there is nothing I can do to repay her for her hospitality towards my family and myself. She always reminded me that everything would be alright and encouraged me to stay focused on God.

Life in prison was a mess, it was like living in hell. The guards were difficult to deal with, they had no respect for anyone at all, neither young nor old. The body search was something I really hated in prison; I hate when a man touched my skin.

Even as a newborn Christian in prison, I received the same treatment like anyone else, except for the chance I had to work inside the studio and host my own program called "Spiritual Upliftment". This was the only privilege I got and it allowed me to be out for a longer period instead of being locked down in my cell. I loved this new gig because it taught me how to keep my mind free despite my body being incarcerated. I enjoyed sharing with my audience in Spanish Town about God's grace and the wonderful things he was doing for us in prison. The people in the community enjoyed the program and gave positive feedback. This was a blessing, a light in a dark place, and it kept me going.

Another thing I detested was that there were no toilets in the cells. What this meant was that if you ever wanted to defecate, you had to do it in a plastic bag and when you are finished you couldn't put it at your feet because another prisoner's head was there. One had no option but to put the feces at your own head and sleep with it overnight. The cell would need to be thoroughly scoured the next day. Some inmates who were in control of a cell, didn't want anyone to ease themselves inside the cell. The worse part was, if you wanted to defecate while someone was cooking, you would be forced to hold it until the cooking was finished, all have eaten and the plates were washed.

The devil was always on the loose in prison. Each day there would be a fight without reason. Anything and everything could be just cause for a fight. I ended up fighting one day as a result of a football game. I was playing behind my dormitory with some other inmates, when a guy hit me smack on my mouth with his elbow and almost knocked my teeth out. The others were upset for what he did and stopped the game. Being a newborn Christian, I wasn't thinking straight and got so angry that I walked over to where he was and punched him in the face. The guard in the century box was watching us the whole time but did not intervene. He knew I wasn't a trouble maker and it was the first time he had seen me in that state; he knew I was a Christian who didn't give trouble and a person who promoted peace at all times.

After the game ended, he decided that the feud wasn't over between us. I was summoned by an officer who was apparently informed that I was involved in a fight. He inquired about what happened between me and this inmate on the football field and I told him. He told me to drop it and that's what I did. I needed to forgive this inmate because the devil was tempting me to do very bad things to him and his crew.

To survive in prison, you must be on your "A" game, because you need to be in top form to stay alive there. I witnessed many persons getting injured and have seen many inmates being beaten by wardens. I was once a very ornery person, but it is this side of me that helped me to survive. Prison is a disgraceful place to be in Jamaica; it can break you and turn you into the most savage person on earth.

There are many ruthless persons in prison harboring a lot of hatred and envy. You receive the ire of other inmates and can be hated for your own possessions or even food. Prison teaches you that all men are equal on the inside because we are all called prisoners, we all are locked in a cell, fed the same food, and the guards treat everyone the same. No one is special in prison and some of the guards are very tough and rigid and can't be bought or sold, that meant your money was useless and any form of treatment was meted out at any time. It was only the light of God that kept me in this dark place.

CHAPTER 13

A Light in a Dark Place

I was angry when the Lord allowed me to go back to prison, but I can say this - it pays to worship God. What He was about to do for me was going to change my life forever. My Pastor kept in touch with me, sometimes we talked, and he would give me encouragement to keep the faith because Jesus Christ was there for me. I was a faithful servant of God in prison, I let my light shine to the other prisoners that they would see and glorify God.

When God favors you, the world will know. That's the reason He said that we should humble ourselves and we will be exalted. What God did for me while in prison caused many to marvel. At one point, God sent two buses with church  members to visit me. I had over thirty visitors at once; it was a joyful moment. We were prohibited from touching outsiders, but the guard allowed me to hug and greet my sisters and brothers in Christ.

Upon observing the jubilant scene, the superintendent called me and asked who I was and why there were so many persons visiting me. I laughed and said, "I'm a child of God, a young preacher". He told me he listened to my radio program, and it was very intriguing, and spirit filled.

More inmates started listening to the radio station since I started the program. Many also started visiting the chapel more frequently on Saturdays since I started preaching there. God was using me, and lives were being transformed. I completed about six months of my four-year sentence before I was granted a transfer to another prison where God showed me favor with some of the wardens and I got a job.

Seven months in, I was back on the street, but now I was working, planting food to help feed the prison population. Life was somewhat easier now that I was at a prison with a shower and toilet inside the dormitory. I could cook my own food and I was in the company of the fairer sex. I eventually changed my job and started working for a private company, earning money, and saving for the day I would be released. I now realized that I had a mission, that I needed to stay focused for Christ because everyone around me was looking to me for leadership.

I became an inspiration not only to prisoners like myself, but also to officers in the prison. I was different from the other prisoners; my life at this point was changing so fast that it amazed me to see how I was being treated by the guards. It almost felt like I was no longer a prisoner. I was free to move around without having any guards watching me. I was even allowed to pick mangoes by myself in the bushes, giving me numerous chances to escape if I wanted to; but I knew those thoughts were of the devil.

Some of the other inmates who worked with me grew jealous of the treatment I was getting, especially from the ladies that I worked with. Some said we were involved romantically in an attempt to assassinate my character. I started finding my purpose by doing ministry on that radio station. Doing God's work became my passion in life and there was no stopping, no pause, even if I had to give up my life. It was the only thing I enjoyed doing since my life was transformed from darkness to light.

My cell phone was very important to me in spreading the gospel of Jesus Christ among the loss souls in the world, but these devices were prohibited. Whenever I got hold of a cell phone, another inmate would make it known to the guard. I was upset and had pernicious thoughts, but I held my peace. I was constantly losing in prison because of envious inmates. It was driving me crazy, and I was becoming bitter because I thought there was no reason for them to rat me out. Then it hit me like a train that God is love and He was teaching me how to love others no matter what my situation was. He was always in control. I only needed to trust and allow Him to take over my life. Love is all about forgiveness, and God had forgiven me of my sins.

Although I wasn't like them, I am surely a sinner who deserved death for my sins. In Luke 11:28 the word of God says, "But He said, yea, rather, blessed are they that hear the word of God and keep it." These words touched my heart, mind and soul deeply; they transformed my life. Now I was studying the word of God and telling others about his goodness and grace; being obedient to my heavenly calling. If God was with me who could be against me? No one.

2 Timothy 2:19 says, "Nevertheless, the foundation of God stands sure, having this seal the Lord knows them that are His, and let everyone that names the name of Christ depart from iniquity". Knowledge of this principle was an integral part to my preparation for the calling of God. Whenever I felt like it was the end of my quest, the Holy Spirit led me to the Bible. There was no other book that so convinced my mind like the inspirational word of God. The Bible is without a rival, it gives peace in believing and a firm hope in the love of GOD. It solves the greatest problems in life and inspires us to live a

life of purity, patience, and goodness. It fills the heart with love for God and a desire to do good to others and thus, prepares us for usefulness here and for a home in heaven.

The Bible also teaches the value of the soul by revealing the price that was paid to redeem us from our sins. It makes known the only antidote for sin and presents the only perfect code of morals ever given. The Bible tells the future and the preparation needed to meet it; it makes us bold for the right things and sustains the soul in adversity and affliction; lighting up dark valleys of death, pointing to a life eternal.

This book led me to God who gives eternal life, the Bible is what keeps me alive. Whenever I got upset with someone, it gave me peace of mind. I read it for comfort and spiritual guidance as the Psalms would say. Psalms 119:18 says, "Open thou mine eyes, that I may behold wonderous things out of thy law". Only when I read God's word can I have a peace of mind. Ephesians 1:17 reminds us that "The God of our Lord Jesus Christ, the father of glory, may give to you the spirit of wisdom and revelation in the knowledge of him".

It is hard to forgive someone that has really done you wrong, because the earthly man always wants revenge. I've always wanted to get even with people who did me wrong, but whenever I read numbers 14:18-20, it reminds of how merciful God is to me – "The Lord is longsuffering and of great mercy, forgiving iniquity and transgression, and by no means clearing the guilty." It gives me a peace of mind to forgive people of the wrong they have done me.

I am not holy; the Bible teaches that we are all filthy rags before God. Romans 3:23 says "For all have sinned and come short of the glory of God." This scripture showed me that not only have I done my fellow men wrong, but I am also a sinner. I have broken the rules of our Creator. God said in the book of Ezekiel 18:4 - "The soul that sins, it shall die." In Romans 5:12 it tells us "Wherefore, as by one man sin entered into the world, and death by sin, and so death passed upon all men, for all have sinned."

CHAPTER 14
The Choice to Serve God

———

God has given us the free will to choose right from wrong, so if we sin willfully after we have received the knowledge of the truth, there remains no more sacrifice for sin but a certain fearful looking for of judgment and fiery indignation which shall devour the adversaries.

I know my God is merciful and forgiving; loving and caring; He wanted me to be a better person for myself and my family. He knew that I had a desire to serve him day and night but there was something still holding me back from giving my heart to him completely. Women were always my weak point and God knew it. I had the desire to have at least five or six women at once because I was afraid of committing to one person, especially after what my ex-girlfriend did to me. My heart was so fond for her, and it really hurt when we broke up. I never thought I would cry daily in my cold prison cell from the emotional pain I felt.

I thought of how we used to share our love with each other; I thought what we had was impeccable. I still feel the same way about her as I did when we first met. I was scared to have a repeat of the same thing I went through with her. God knows we are not perfect beings; make mistakes at times; so, laugh at your troubles but learn from them.

As a baptized Christian I strive for perfection in holiness. I knew that if my ex was the one that God created for me, then He would put us back together and no one could separate us. It was pain and distress that brought me to God; my life has never been easy. However, I knew for a fact that I was placed on earth to make a difference in people's lives.

Whenever I read the newspaper, watched television, or listened to the radio, there were so many crime stories, war, and terrorism. If you think about your own troubles, perhaps illness or the death of a loved one, it causes you great distress and you may even feel like the good man Job, filled with dishonor and affliction. Sometimes you ask yourself - Is this God's purpose for me and for the rest of humanity? Where can I get help to cope with my problems? Is there any hope that we will ever see peace on earth? These are questions that I asked God.

The Holy Spirit led me to God's word which provided the answers I sought. "And God will wipe away every tear from their eyes; there shall be no more death, nor sorrow, nor crying. There shall be no more pain, for the former things have passed away" (Revelation 21:4). "Then the eyes of the blind shall be opened, and the ears of the deaf shall be unstopped. Then the lame shall leap like a deer, and the tongue of the dumb sing" (Isaiah 35:5,6).

Jehovah will give us peace and abundant joy and I know these to be true. I still find myself in deep thought at times and doubting, despite knowing the truth. The truth just hard for me to accept at times, especially in times of fierce trials. There was a time when an inmate consistently provoked me, and went as far as making a weapon that he claimed was for me. Why? I prevented him from using my phone because he treated others unfairly. He professed to be Muslim. He would laugh whenever I worshipped Jesus; he really tested my faith to the point where I wanted to beat the dust off him, but the Holy Spirit would not allow me to.

That demon wanted to destroy my life but I knew that every believing soul should conform entirely to God's will and remain on a path of repentance and contrition, exercising faith in the atoning merits of the Redeemer, and advancing in strength. My quest with the Lord was fabulous, God constantly showed me that He is loving and caring, merciful and forgiving. He was preparing me to lead the vulnerable youth back to His path of righteousness; all I needed to do was be obedient to His word and my blessings would follow.

I started pondering nature itself and learned many potent lessons. I looked at the eagle how they flew alone and at high altitude, and I told myself that I needed to stay away from narrow-minded people who didn't believe in Christ and are trying to bring me down. Eagles also have accurate vision, so I needed keep my eyes on the work of the Lord and remain focused regardless of the situation or obstacles I faced each day.

My plight in prison was not an easy road, but I knew that God would give me fortitude on my quest to overcome the obstacles I faced in my life. I laughed at my mistakes but I learned from them as well. I faced my difficulties with joy but I overcome them; joked about my troubles but took strength from them. By the love of Jesus Christ, I overcame all my obstacles. We need Jesus as our Lord and Savior in this sinful world. How many of us have assured interest in Jesus Christ? The term assure means guaranteed, certain and secure; how interested are we in Jesus Christ? How real is the Son of God to us?

There is no better way to awaken our drowsy conscience, than to surrender to Jesus. "I beseech you therefore, brethren, by the mercies of God, that you present your bodies a living sacrifice, holy, acceptable to God, which is your reasonable service." (Romans 12:1). "Therefore, if anyone is in Christ, he is a new creation; old things have passed away; behold, all things have become new." (2 Corinthians 5:17). The Bible tells me that once I accept Jesus Christ as my personal Savior, I am a new person. The devil wasn't about to stand down, he knew I was one of his lieutenants and now I became a five-star general for Christ. He tried using his charm and charisma on me to carry out his duty and sent temptations of women, cars, and money.

I wasn't about to give in so easily because Jesus Christ, the Son of God had paid the ransom for my sins. Children of God are called to be representatives of Christ, showing faith, goodness, love and mercy that Christ has revealed to us. We are to reveal the character of Christ to a world that doesn't know Him. "As You sent Me into the world, I also have sent them into the world." (John 17:18). I was convicted that Jesus is the way the truth and the life. Some say there is neither God nor heaven, but I am not believing the lie. Think about it? Why go through hell, die, and go to hell for the hell of it? That's too much hell for me. If we will only accept that we are sinners before God and confess our sins to Him, "He is faithful and just to forgive us our sins and to cleanse us from all unrighteousness." (1 John 1:9).

As I get older, I have started to understand that common sense isn't so common after all. I've learned that not everyone believes in Jesus Christ as the Son of God and Creator. Some are atheists, agnostics, and some are believers; it's a mixed bag, but Jesus died for us all. Praise God! I can boast in my Lord Jesus as my Savior. "For what man knows the things of a man except the spirit of the man which is in him? Even so no one knows the things of God except the Spirit of God. Now we have received, not the spirit of the world, but the Spirit who is from God, that we might know the things that have been freely given to us by God." (1 Corinthians 2:11-12).

As a Christian, if I say that I have fellowship with Jesus Christ and walk in darkness, I'm a liar. "But if we walk in the light as He is in the light, we have fellowship with one another, and the blood of Jesus Christ His Son cleanses us from all sin." (1 John 1:7). Your heart may feel down at times due to the things you have to face in your daily life, but I learnt that no one can block the blessings that God has in store for you. On my bad days I seek the Lord, on my good days I thank Him, on my excellent moments I praise him, but every day I need Him. Thank you, Lord for always being there for me!

Each day I pray that the Lord will strengthen my mind, body, and spirit when I feel weary. I pray that the Lord refresh my thoughts when I feel afraid, and make me courageous and strong. I will walk in complete confidence and faith, knowing that the Lord is with me every step of the way. I was such a nincompoop, destroying my life and taking others with me at the same time; but God had another plan for me – to win souls for his kingdom through my testimony.

First, God had to put me somewhere where I would completely give Him my attention and cry out my heart to Him. My plight was so severe that it was impossible for a natural man to overcome on his own. Jehovah started to teach me about his handy work and how amazing the world He created was. Besides the marvelous creatures, there were many other examples of amazing life that could be explored.

The production of light by the firefly; the generation of electricity by the electric eel; the ability of the bat to navigate in the dark using echo location; the transformation of a caterpillar into a butterfly; and many other wonders spoke to God's creative power. We don't often consider the kind of world that is needed for life to thrive. As scientists have explored our universe, they have become more and more aware of how unique and well-designed our world is. They see more and more what exact and special conditions are needed if life is going to survive.

Earth itself was carefully designed for life, with the exact combination of environmental conditions, a suitable source of energy such as sun light, raw materials for constructing cells and tissues, nutrients, etc. The universe was intelligently and purposefully planned.

Many scientists have commented on the precise features of our universe and concluded that they appear to be the result of intelligent planning. The best explanation and the one that fits what we see is that it was intentionally created by one with unlimited power and intelligence. I sat down and pondered on how awesome God is and thanked Him for creating me and granting me the privilege to speak about his righteousness and all the kindness that He showed me, even when I fell short of His glory.

God has given me the greatest gift one could ever dream of - the ransom of His only Son, Jesus Christ, for our sins. Remember that a gift doesn't have to be expensive to be important. After all, the true value of a gift is not necessarily measured in terms of money, rather, when a gift brings you happiness or fills a need in your life, it has value to you. Of the many gifts you could ever hope to receive, there is one that stands out above all the others - it is a gift from God to mankind.

Among the many things He has given to us, His greatest gift to us was the ransom sacrifice of his son Jesus Christ. Read Matthew 20:28 - "Even as the son of man come not to be ministered unto, but to minister and to give his life a ransom for many". We see in this chapter that this ransom was the most valuable gift we could possibly receive for brings untold happiness and can fill our most important needs. It is really the greatest expression of God's love for us.

"In whom we have redemption through His blood, the forgiveness of sins, according to the riches of His grace." (Ephesians 1:7). To grasp the meaning of this Bible teaching, we only need to think back to what happened in the garden of Eden. Only when we understand what the man and the woman lost when they sinned in the garden of Eden, can we appreciate why Jesus' sacrifice is such an invaluable gift unto us now.

When God created Adam, He gave him something truly precious - a perfect life on earth. Consider what that meant for Adam; he was made with a perfect body and mind. He didn't know sickness, aging or death. As a perfect human being he had a special relationship with God. Luke 3:38 tells us that he was considered a son of God – "Which was the son of Enos, which was the son of Seth, which was the son of Adam, which was the son of God". Being made in God's image meant that Adam was created with characteristics like those of God, including love, wisdom, justice and even immortality. Adam also possessed free will; hence he wasn't like a machine that performed only what it is designed or programmed to do. Instead, he could make personal decisions, choosing between right and wrong.

If Adam had chosen to obey God, he would have lived forever in paradise on earth; but he, being disobedient to God, made life on earth very difficult. I am at times disobedient to God, but because He is merciful, His arms are always open for me to come back to Him. In Isaiah 48:17-18 God said to us – "I am, the Lord your God, who teaches you to profit, who leads you by the way you should go, oh, that you had heeded my commandments, then your peace would have been like a river, and your righteousness like the waves of the sea". All these He wants to give us if we obey Him.

I was in tears as He revealed His love to me in His word. My heart became contrite within me to see how disobedient I was to a loving God. Ezekiel 33:11 reminds us that God's discipline has always flowed from a heart of love to protect his children from sin's fatal force. God takes no pleasure in the death of the wicked.

When we are disobedient to God, we face sorrow in our daily lives. Jeremiah 2:17-19 says "Have you not brought this on yourself in that you have forsaken the Lord your God when he led you in the way? Your own wickedness will correct you, and your backslidings will rebuke you." When sinners die, it is the direct consequence of their own choice. When we commit sin, we are not cast off without mercy; we have hope and he opportunity to repent in faith in the Lord Jesus.

Through faith, I was transformed from a child of sin to a loyal subject of Jesus Christ; not because of an inherent goodness but because of the goodness of Christ who provides forgiveness of sins. His sacrifice fulfilled the demands of justice. God's boundless mercy is exercised toward those who are wholly undeserving. We must, at all times, pray and ask God's forgiveness of our sins; but we are often deterred by our ignorance and self-centeredness.

Some people fail to acknowledge Jesus Christ as their Lord and Savior, but it is important that we remember that when we die in sin, there is no repentance in the grave. We should fear God out of loving heart towards Him (Acts 17:30-31). In times of ignorance, God overlooks our shortcomings, but commands all men everywhere to repent, because He has appointed a day in which He will judge the world in righteousness.

CHAPTER 15
It Pays to Fear God

————

The Bible shows us that we should fear God who created us. He created us for a reason, that is to worship and praise Him. But we tend to have our own way at times and allow the darkness of the devil to overshadow us. As followers of Christ, we must turn away from fleshly lusts and take up our cross and follow Jesus. We must be obedient, but the flesh is always in conflict with the Spirit of God; praying always for strength to push forward in the faith. The devil knows that he only has a short time before the judgment of God is upon the earth. Satan is seeking to devour souls and destroy lives, but I am here to proclaim that Jesus Christ came that you may have life and have it more abundantly.

Take it from me, peace in this life can't be yours until you accept Jesus Christ as your personal Savior. My life isn't an easy road, I am not a perfect man nor am I a holy man of God, but I can tell you this, each time I fall from God's grace I go down on my knees in prayer asking Him for forgiveness for all my sins. Just bear in mind that I was once an outcast to the church.

When I was unrepentant of my sins and did not accept Jesus Christ, others looked down on me as if I was a savage. This made me furious inside my heart towards these people; my heart was as hard as a stone. I just wanted to see blood all day, every day, as long as it wasn't mine. Deep down I always wanted to find a church to attend; my desire was always to worship and praise God.

I knew that my habits were contrary to the will of God. I once was lost in sin and enjoyed it. I lusted in my heart for beautiful women, always wanting to have more than one woman in my life at once. Deep inside my heart I knew my actions were wrong.

Reflecting on my life, it reminds me of what Paul said – "For I know that in me (that is, in my flesh) dwells no good thing: for to will is present with me, but how to perform that which is good I find not. For the good I wish to do, I don't: but the evil which I wish not to do, that I do. Now, if I do what I don't wish to do, it is no more I that do it, but sin that dwelleth in me. For I delight in the law of God after the inward man: But I see another law in my members warring against the law of my mind, and bringing me into captivity to the law of sin which is in my members. O wretched man that I am! who shall deliver me from the body of this death?"

I thank God through Jesus Christ my Lord for working on me, so now, I'm serving and worshiping His holy name. My sins were against the law of God, but through His love and grace, I have been going through much change in my life – physically, spiritually, emotionally, and mentally. For the glory of God, my experiences were to make me into the man He wanted to be. I had to face all the challenges, to become strong in the Lord. Now I feel as solid as a rock in my faith and in the word of God. I rejoice every day for the second chance He has given me to seek his loving mercy and grace, knowing that when I was shot in my face, twice, I could have died. God give me a second chance to make my wrongs right.

In the grave there is no repentance of sin. When I read Philippians 4:4-7, it puts a smile on my face; it says – "Rejoice in the Lord always; and again, I say, rejoice. Let your moderation be known to all men. The Lord is at hand. Do not be anxious about anything but in everything by prayer and supplication with thanksgiving, let your request be made known to God and the peace of God which passes all understanding shall keep your hearts and minds through Jesus Christ". God loves me and wants me to have a full and complete life in Him, a life of joy and not of despair. He wants me to know that His love is never ending. He is great in mercy, cleansing our iniquities and clearing the guilty.

My life of imprisonment was a time of learning. There were many times when other inmates provoked me to wrath, like using profane words to me and stealing my belongings. I often asked God why He was allowing me to be treated this way by fools? I must admit, I was really being prepared by Almighty God to do the things that He required of me. I was being readied to minister in His mighty name among sinners for the glory of His heavenly kingdom.

Today, I am confident in telling people about my past life and how the grace of God helped me to overcome all the stumbling blocks I faced. "Wherefore gird up the lions of your mind, be sober, and hope to the end for the grace that is to be brought unto you at the revelation of Jesus Christ. As obedient children not fashioning yourselves according to the former lusts in your ignorance: But as he which hath called you is holy, so be ye holy in all manner of conversation." (1 Peter 1: 13-16).

Whenever you read this powerful Bible verse ask God to bring your mind into holiness; ask Him to bring your heart and mind into unity with His holiness. Ask him to pour out His Spirit of knowledge, wisdom, and understanding upon you. When you meditate on what the Spirit of wisdom and knowledge reveals to you and see how unworthy and filthy you are in the sight of a holy God, you should thank the Lord for each day that he sustains you with His breath of life.

I came to the realization that although we are filthy rags in the sight of the Lord, He loves us so much that He will not destroy us without giving us a chance to repent of our sins. God is jealous and just. He makes it to rain on the just and on the unjust alike. "For by grace are we saved through faith, and that not of yourselves it is the gift of God not of work lest any, man should boast." (Ephesians 2:8-9). This verse demonstrates His love for sinners because when we sin, it continues to awaken us to the truth, and He gives us that second chance to repent of our sins. Please pay close attention to what I am saying about sin. God doesn't love sin; He has made it clear in His word. He told the man and the woman in Genesis 2:17 – "In the day that thou eat thereof thou shall surely die." Sin leads to death. "The soul that sins it shall die." (Ezekiel 18:4). God loves you and me, but he hates sin.

Look at how our holy God demonstrated his love for us; Romans 5:8 tells us – "But God commends his love towards us, in that while we were yet sinners Christ died for us." It isn't always easy to live a Christ-like life, but God has given us the fortitude to overcome whatever we face daily, because the blood of His son, Jesus Christ, covers us from all evil that we face in our daily lives.

The Bible teaches us in 1 Peter 1:18-19 – "For as much as you know that you were not redeemed with corruptible things as silver and gold, from your vain conversation received by tradition from your fathers: but with the precious blood of Christ, as of a lamb without blemish and without spot." Your mind is the compass of your life, it convicts us of how filthy we are in the sight of God. Praise the Lord! Jesus stepped in and His blood cleanses us from all our sins.

CHAPTER 16

A Praying and Supportive Church

I always knew that a lot of righteous people were praying for me to be a mighty man of God. A mighty woman of Christ was always praying on my behalf, that God would touch me from the crown of my head to the sole of my feet with His blessings. She was like my mentor and motivated me to live for Christ Jesus. Always supportive, her love and kindness gave me fortitude on this quest to redemption in Christ.

I now strive for spiritual purity daily and positive progression in every aspect of my life. The love and encouragement that I have received are priceless; the kind that money can't afford; this is the love Christ speaks about. I love this lady like my mother; she is a spiritual guide in my life whenever I am going through hard situations. Her shoulders are always there for me to cry on.

Pastor Charles Brevitt was one of the spiritual leaders of the church who saw that God was going to use me for His glory and that I would win dying souls for the kingdom of God. He placed His angels around me to give me strength in times of need.

My mother and family members always stood by my side in times of need as much as my church family did. I must confess that I believe God has angels in the church. There was this lady – Mrs. Brown who was present the very night I got saved. I have never seen an angel before, but I know that this woman is an angel sent from God to do missionary work for the kingdom. She was like a mother in the manner in which she treated me; there are no words deep enough, or fine enough, or sweet enough to explain how I love this lady.

I must say God has placed some genuine souls around me also, people that I can call upon in times of need. My life has never felt so easy until I gave my life to Christ Jesus. 2 Timothy 2:19 says - "Nevertheless the solid foundation of God stands, having this seal: "The Lord knows those who are His," and, "Let everyone who names the name of Christ depart from iniquity." Whenever I read this Bible verse it reminds me that the foundation of Christ stands sure. The moment I accepted Jesus as my Savior I found life eternal. "In him was life and the life was the light of man." (John 1:4).

There is nothing else in this world than can convince the mind but the inspiration of the word of God. Whenever I'm down and I read the Bible, it gives me inner peace. The Bible is without   rival, it gives a calm in believing and a firm hope in the future.

It solves the greatest problems and inspires to a life of purity. It fills the heart with love for God and a desire to do good to others while preparing us for usefulness here and in the life to come. It teaches the value of the soul by revealing the price that has been paid to redeem it. "For ye are bought with a price, therefore glorify God in your body, and in your spirit which are God's." (1 Corinthians 6:20).

"Christ hath redeemed us from the curse of the law, being made a curse for us: for it is written cursed is everyone that hangs on a tree." (Galatians 3:13). "Knowing that you were not redeemed with corruptible things, like silver or gold, from your aimless conduct received by tradition from your fathers, but with the precious blood of Christ, as of a lamb without blemish and without spot." (1 Peter1:18-19). The Bible is God's gift to us mankind, it contains the character and mind of God.

God's love for you and all people was revealed when Jesus came into the world as a human being, lived a sinless life, died on the cross and rose from the dead. The Bible is my guide for how to live a God-fearing life here on earth. Whenever I fall into temptation, it strengthens me and encourages me to live a peaceful and righteous life in the sight of a holy God.

Along my journey, it taught me patience and love, making me more relaxed and not easily disturbed. There were times when people to great lengths to fabricate lies and mar my integrity, but I am now able to say that when these trials come my way, I pray that God gives me that same type of faith that Job had to overcome in perilous times.

CHAPTER 17
God's Mouthpiece

———

In March 2018 while at the Tamarind Farm Correctional Institution, I applied for parole after completing about one third of my four-year sentence. In facing my trials in jail, I sometimes wanted to let them have the wrath of my hands, because deep down I knew that these prisoners were deserving of what I would unleash. I often asked myself – if Judas had sold out Jesus Christ who is sinless, for thirty pieces of silver, what won't they do to a sinner like myself? As a Christian who was no longer living for the things of the world, I knew it was God who was keeping through all the trials I faced.

God is seeking to make Himself known to us and bring us into communion with Him. Even through nature, He speaks to our senses ceaselessly. The open heart will be impressed with the love and glory of God as revealed through the works of his hands. If we listen, we can hear and understand the communications of God through the things of nature such as the rain, green forests, the sun, moon, wind, the vast ocean and the creatures therein. We are invited to become acquainted with God, our Creator.

God speaks to us through His providential workings and through the influence of His spirit upon our hearts. We may find precious lessons if our hearts are open to God to discern them.

If the other prisoners who provoked me were putting the same energy into asking God for forgiveness of their sins, their lives would be stress free through the love of God and the redemptive love of Jesus Christ. The Bible teaches that Jesus paid the penalty for all your sins. Christ loved us enough to die for us even when we were rebelling against him. I would like you to pay close attention to what the Bible says about our loving Savior in Romans 5:1-2 - "Therefore being justified by faith we have peace with God through our Lord Jesus Christ: by whom also we have access by faith into his grace wherein we stand and rejoice in hope of the glory of God." TO GOD BE THE GLORY!

Many of the inmates did not believe in God at all. They denied that Jesus Christ is the son of God and the coming Savior of humanity. Some even used profanity against Christ. The psalmist wrote in Psalms 139:19-24 – "O, that You would slay the wicked, O God! Depart from me, you bloodthirsty men. For they speak against You wickedly; Your enemies take Your name in vain. Do I not hate them, O Lord, who hate You? And do I not loathe those who rise up against You? I hate them with perfect hatred; I count them my enemies. Search me, O God, and know my heart;

Try me, and know my thoughts; and see if there is any wicked way in me, and lead me in the way everlasting."

When I heard these inmates cursing God and attacking me every single day, I thanked God because it was evidence that I had reached a higher plain; higher ground. "Therefore, I endure all things for the elect's sake, that they may obtain the salvation which is in Christ Jesus with eternal glory. It is a faithful saying: for if we be dead with Him, we shall also live with Him, if we suffer, we shall also reign with Him: if we deny Him, He also will deny us. If we are faithless, He remains faithful; He cannot deny Himself." (2 Timothy 2:10-13). Most of the inmates who were at the Tamarind Farm Correctional Institution didn't believe in God, but He opened my eyes like an Eagle so that I could see them.

"The Lord has made all for Himself, Yes, even the wicked for the day of doom. Everyone who is proud in heart is an abomination to the Lord; Though they join forces, none will go unpunished." (Proverbs 16:4-5). "The tongue of the wise uses knowledge rightly, But the mouth of fools pours forth foolishness." (Proverbs 15:2). You see, God was teaching me the signs of the wicked. Prison was the perfect place to learn. I needed to be humbled so that I could become fit to do God's work.

"Pride goes before destruction, and a haughty spirit before a fall." (Proverbs 16:18). This is profound teaching. I tell you the truth, if those prisoners would only acknowledge Jesus Christ as their Savior and repent of their sins, life would be a blessing to them. Rather, they chose to live in sin and worship the devil who is their master. I realized that Jesus wanted me to go through trials and tribulation to see how strong my faith was in Him. God is long suffering my people, and of great mercy, forgiving iniquity and transgression.

The scriptures serve to keep us focused and always reminded that our God is of never-ending mercy, one who will forgive us of your sins if we confess them to him and ask forgiveness. "If we confess our sins, he is faithful and just to forgive us our sins, and to cleanse us from all unrighteousness." (1 John 1:9). As human beings everything we do seems right unto us until someone proves us wrong. The Bible says in Proverbs 14:12 - "There is a way which seems right to a man, but the end thereof are the ways of death." The more I read God's word, the fonder my heart grew towards people whom I once considered enemies. His word always convicted me of my past record of the man I once was.

When you become a Christian, your life has to be changed completely, you have to display the attributes of Christ which are love, joy, peace etc. Christians must live by every word that proceeds out of the mouth of God; we are to believe in and live in Christ who is the way, the truth, and the life. Yes, my carnal mind wanted revenge for the things that some of those inmates did to me, but the word of God said those of the flesh do the things of the flesh, and those of the spirit do the things of the spirit. Jesus said, "Behold, I stand at the door and knock. If anyone hears My voice and opens the door, I will come in to him and dine with him, and he with Me. To him who overcomes I will grant to sit with Me on My throne, as I also overcame and sat down with My Father on His throne." (Revelation 3:20-21).

Christ was showing me that as long as I believe in Him, I can overcome anything, because "He who is in [me] is greater than he who is in the world." (1 John 4:4). Prayer is a powerful weapon. Whenever I find myself in despair, I go down on my knees in prayer to God and He always delivers; He has never failed me not once. I overcame tribulation and humiliating situations which I faced daily without getting myself into physical altercations with anyone. This was a sign that God placed a canopy over me. I now know that there is power in the name of Jesus to break curses of despair. I believe and I proclaim in the mighty name of Jesus Christ that every demonic weapon that revolts against me shall perish.

CHAPTER 18

A Soldier in God's Army

———

God wants men of valor in his army, not foot soldiers. I am a warrior for Him, pushing forward by any means to attain victory in Jesus Christ, for He's the one who gives me fortitude and my quest for victory. I can testify to the world that there is power in the name of Jesus. When you call on Him, the devil and his followers tremble in fear. I know that God favored me because no matter how my character was attacked, He didn't allow them to triumph over me. I resided in prison, but my mind was ever on my Creator and His word. I feared God, not man, for man can only destroy my flesh, nothing else. I separated myself from the wolves, but trouble continued to find me, but nothing can take me off this path with Christ.

I had a vision once that my soul was burning in hell, and I cried aloud to God to forgive me of my sins, then something happened - I woke up, I was so elated to know it was just a dream. God was telling me that He was not pleased with my lifestyle, and I needed to repent of my sins. If I had died in my sins that would certainly mean hell for me.

Paul, a faithful servant of Christ, had worked out his salvation with fear and trembling. Should we not fear so that we avoid falling short of the promise that was left us and prove ourselves worthy of eternal life?

God bestowed upon me the knowledge of his word and granted me the privilege of becoming a partaker of his divine nature. This is the highest honor, the greatest joy possible for Him to give to humanity. Those who become participants in this labor of love are brought close to their Creator. We must always strive for spiritual purity and positive progression daily and in every aspect of our lives. I try my best not to allow the 'slime' to enter my surrounding or my system; only those who strive for the same things are the ones that I embrace whole heartedly. We should, with prayer, strive with organizing efforts to enter in at the narrow gate that leads to heaven.

Many of the prisoners were obstinate when it came to learning about Jesus, so God gave them over to turmoil. God calls fools, but he doesn't keep them in that state. He is merciful and forgiving, always with open arms to receive every sinner that confesses their sins to Him. I learned how to be content in whatever state I am. What I went through in life and overcame, prepared me to be a better minister for

Christ; it is my joy to tell others about God's loving and saving grace.

What a perfect gift that God has given to us! One that money can't buy - the precious blood of Jesus Christ that takes away all sins. God gave His son as a ransom for our sins. "For you are bought with a price, therefore glorify God in your body and in your spirit which are God's." (Corinthians 6:20). "Christ has redeemed us from the curse of the law, being made a curse for us: for it is written, cursed is everyone that hangs on a tree." (Galatians 3:13). "Neither by the blood of goats and calves, but by his own blood he entered in once into the holy place, having obtained eternal redemption for us." (Hebrews 9:12).

This was God's gift to us to bring us back into communion with himself, salvation is a free gift from God to us, but I tell you, it cannot be yours until you freely accept that Jesus Christ is your Lord and Savior. "Knowing that you were not redeemed with corruptible things, like silver or gold, from your aimless conduct received by tradition from your fathers, 19 but with the precious blood of Christ, as of a lamb without blemish and without spot." (1 Peter 1:18-19). As I sit and ponder on these Bible verses, I know for a fact, how merciful God really is towards us. For every new day I give thanks to Him to be alive.

Sometimes my quest became so difficult that I just wanted to kill someone to appease my ego; but then I'd ask myself - Is this the character of Christ? Is this what Christ would do? My brothers and sisters in Christ, it is not easy to overcome the devil when you lose focus on Christ. All the worldly things that you have set aside resurfaces in your mind and tempts you to do evil. It is so easy to do the wrong rather than right.

I tell you these things because anyone who reads my story can never be the same again after reading of my life's quest as a baptized Christian. I have fallen short of God's glory more than once. My heart felt contrite as I put pen to paper and started writing about my life. Rest assured that every word that I have written herein are authentic, honest and true.

CHAPTER 19

Reflections

———

Let me take you back a little in my life to make a few things clear to you about my journey. Leading up to accepting Jesus as my Savior, I was a quiet young man growing up with my mother and her family, until my mother sent me off to live with my paternal relatives in Spanish Town, St. Catherine. I lived with my grandparents, aunts and uncles. During this time, I was quite slow in school and my aunts would beat me every day to spell words which I had difficulty in spelling. Being a seven-year-old child at the time, I wasn't allowed to eat until I learned to spell every single word that I was given. I literacy started improving after two years of hard training from my aunts.

A grave mistake was made when my father made the decision to bring me back to my mother's side of the family, because this was where my life started becoming complicated. As a child, I was growing up in a very inimical community with crime all around me every day. It became easy for me to adapt to the lifestyle around me. I wanted to get involved in the things I saw the older boys do.

I wanted to drink alcohol too because I was getting a taste of it from time to time. I started smoking marijuana and thinking it was helping me to become a gangster, but in reality, it was messing up my little mind from an early stage. If adults find it hard to manage alcohol, how could a child do it? I eventually started stealing my mom's used cigarettes, hiding and smoking them with my friends. The mentality I had as a child was really messed up.

There was no one to guide and direct me in the path a child should go. The older I became, the more exposure I got to criminal activities in my youthful days and I was enjoying them, because I didn't know better at the time. As a juvenile, everything that I did seemed good to me. There were a few teachers I didn't like in school as a child, and my attitude was not indicative of what we want in schools from children. My behavior started creating problems for both parents and teachers alike; I was acting like the teacher instead of the student.

When a child creates problems in a class, it is hard for teachers to concentrate on what he or she is teaching. My behavior not only caused problems for the teachers, but also created problems for the other kids to learn what the teacher was trying to teach them.

Sometimes when children act out of character, it is not due to a lack of proper home training because parents can do all the necessary things required of them, but the child, when away from home, can be influenced to act in ways that will blow your mind as an adult. 'Bad company' is never a good thing, especially at a tender age. I believe that every child should experience the rod of correction and a little military training to help guide them in the right path. Children often do things out of curiosity, but are ignorant to the fact that smoking, drinking, sex and crime will only lead to destruction.

I have experienced many things in my personal life, so I can say without a doubt that a lot of the blame placed on parents is undeserved. Many parents are totally innocent and shouldn't be blamed for what their children do in the street; believe me. Sometimes I cry as an adult to see all the heartache I put my mother through in the short time I've been on earth. Experiences don't always teach you wisdom because some things are just plain spiritual that only the Holy Spirit can teach you. An ignorant person thinks everything he or she does is right in his or her own sight, until the Holy Spirit starts teaching them spiritual things and they start seeing their earthly flaws.

Today, I stand firm, grounded and steadfast in the faith and can testify of the wondrous, unequivocal, unmerited love, mercy and grace of God. Jesus, My Lord, did it for me; He transformed and set me free from evil. He did it for me and I know, without a doubt, that He will do it for you too.

THE CONCLUSION

———

"Let us hear the conclusion of the whole matter: Fear God and keep His commandments, for this is the whole duty of mankind. For God will bring every work into judgement, including every secret thing, whether good or evil."
-Ecclesiastes 12:13, 14

THE EXHORTATION

———

"Seek the Lord while He may be found, call on Him while He is near. Let the wicked forsake his way, and the unrighteous man his thoughts; let him return to the Lord, and He will have mercy on Him; and to our God, for He will abundantly pardon."
- Isaiah 55:6,7

THE INVITATION

———

"Behold, I stand at the door and knock. If anyone hears My voice and opens the door, I will come in to him and dine with Him, and he with Me. To him who overcomes I will grant to sit with Me on My throne..."
-Revelation 3:20,21

Reach out to the author for feedback, bookings, and orders:
campbellmilton415@gmail.com

40517787R00079